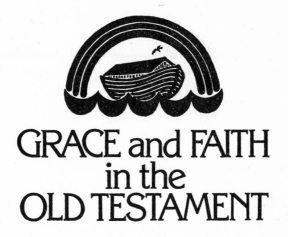

GRACE and FAITH
in the
OLD TESTAMENT

GRACE AND FAITH IN THE OLD TESTAMENT

Ronald M. Hals

AUGSBURG Publishing House • Minneapolis

GRACE AND FAITH IN THE OLD TESTAMENT

CONTENTS

INTRODUCTION

"By grace you have been saved through faith" (Eph. 2:8).
Those are big words, especially for Protestant Christians. They
summarize our Reformation heritage, but we didn't get them
from the Reformation. They came to us *via* the Reformers, but
they constitute a rediscovery by the Reformers of a basic emphasis of the New Testament itself. Of course, this stress on
"by grace . . . through faith" is not equally prominent in all
the New Testament writings. We're fully aware that the Gospels don't present Jesus as using that language. Naturally not,
for "by grace . . . through faith" is the particular theological
language that came out of the conflict of the Apostle Paul with
the so-called Judaizers. Over against these Judaizers, who
insisted that Paul's Gentile converts would have to observe
certain Old Testament laws such as circumcision, before they
could become Christians, Paul maintained that entry into the

Christian church came not by any "works" of the law but by grace through faith. His letter to the Romans and especially that to the Galatians make plain the background theological quarrel out of which the formula "by grace . . . through faith" developed.

In the Gospel tradition, Jesus doesn't face that situation. He didn't talk about Gentile converts to Christianity having trouble with Judaizers. That situation didn't develop until decades later, and it came not in Palestine but in Galatia. Still, that does not mean that the Gospels stand in opposition to the theology of "by grace . . . through faith." Far from it! Although the particular theological words may not be present, the same realities are there. No one would want to claim that just because certain words are absent the ideas are missing. After all, grace and faith are not just words, they are realities, deeper realities than any particular set of words. It is the Apostle Paul's claim that they are part and parcel of God's revealing of himself. In line with that emphasis, the Reformation affirms that grace and faith sum up the center of that revelation in the entire Bible.

Well, the Bible includes both Old and New Testaments, and it is the Christian claim that it is the same God who reveals himself in both Testaments. The very presence of the Old Testament in the Christian canon is an affirmation that the Hebrew Scriptures are more than a useful historical background. They were, after all, the Bible of the early church, the sacred writings quoted by the New Testament writers. Clearly for the apostolic witnesses, it was not just the case that God's revelation in Jesus illuminated the meaning of the Old Testament. These men made extensive use of those Old Testament Scriptures in order to show how they shed a light on what God was doing in Jesus. For them, the illumination went both ways! In particular the Apostle Paul took sizable pains to assert that his message of salvation by grace through faith was in direct continuity with the Jewish Scriptures. In fact, it is especially in connection with this central part of his theology that he argues in great detail in Romans 4 and Galatians 3 that already in Abraham salvation came precisely by grace and through faith rather than by works of the law.

Quite clearly Paul's Judaizing opponents felt they were the ones who were being true to the Old Testament heritage. Doubtless they would have viewed Paul's arguments about Abraham as ingenious but unconvincing. Very strangely, many Christians seem to have felt the Judaizers were right about this. For reasons to be explored later, many of Paul's heirs believe that the message of salvation by grace through faith stands in sharp contrast to the message of the Old Testament. In highest irony it has been especially among Lutherans, those who have traditionally given greatest prominence to the Pauline message, that this actually anti-Pauline view has been found.

It will be my contention here that the Apostle Paul was not wrong. I shall show that already in the Old Testament salvation came by grace through faith. But, rather than simply opposing one conclusion to another, let us look at the disputed evidence, the Old Testament itself. Actually, all that is necessary is to listen faithfully and carefully to the material and the facts will make themselves clear. At the very least, in view of the central importance of the issue and the sharpness of the differences involved, the investigation should be an exciting one!

A word about the plan of this book will perhaps be helpful at this point. The discussion that follows could be divided into three parts: Shape, Settings, and Summary.

Chapter 1 presents the shape or definition of the question.

Chapters 2 through 5 present the various settings of God's

gracious activity. By "setting" I mean the locale, the context or environment of ideas, within which the subjects of grace and faith are encountered. In the New Testament you hear Paul talk about "by grace" and "through faith" within a polemical context, in opposition to the insistence of Judaizers that Gentiles had to fulfill certain requirements of Old Testament law before they could become Christians. A clear understanding of that setting greatly aids one's efforts at comprehending precisely what grace and faith mean. It is of similar help in seeking to grasp the significance of grace and faith in the Old Testament if one can have a clear picture of the context within which these twin subjects are usually encountered. Actually, there are four such settings which play prominent roles in the Hebrew Bible, and we shall examine each of them individually in Chapters 2 through 5.

The summary is provided in Chapter 6.

1

LISTENING TO
THE OLD TESTAMENT

BEFORE WE CAN LOOK either carefully or faithfully at what is presented about both grace and faith in the Old Testament, some preliminary clarification is vital. Essentially there is only one prerequisite for effective listening, and that is to allow the material to speak on its own terms. The example already touched on of the place of grace and faith in the Gospels is a good case in point. We naturally do not expect the explicit vocabulary of salvation by grace through faith and apart from the works of the law to characterize the Synoptic Gospels, for that vocabulary arose as part of a dispute later than the life of Jesus. Nevertheless, this does not mean it is irrelevant to ask about grace and faith in the synoptics.

Such an investigation would be appropriate for two reasons:

First, because the actual writing of these Gospels took place at a time after the problem arose with the Judaizers and, because both the writers and the audience of the Gospels were people who had lived through this and other doctrinal struggles of the church's early history, one might expect that the way in which the Gospel tradition was preserved might well reflect something of the heritage of this controversy. Even if the words of Jesus were preserved inviolate, the work of the tradition-preservers in selecting and presenting those words could quite possibly reveal the effects of the intervening controversy.

Second, and more important, if grace and faith are not just words but deep and important theological realities, then it would only be expectable that an attitude or position about the realities themselves should appear, even though likely in a different setting and with a different vocabulary.

To examine biblical literature in this way, that is by listening to it speak within its own setting is effective listening. The alternative of demanding that material from one setting should be expected to speak from the perspective of another setting, is simply to refuse to take its setting seriously. To conclude that the Gospels do not endorse salvation by grace through faith because Jesus' words don't even employ this terminology would be obvious folly. Similarly, it makes no sense to approach the Old Testament by asking, "Where is anything said about salvation by grace through faith?" Just as a responsible approach to the Gospel tradition, both the sayings of Jesus and the witness of the Evangelists, would have to begin by taking into account the shape or form of the material itself, so a similar approach is a must for coming to look at the Old Testament on this same issue.

The discipline of form criticism has brought about tremendous progress by steadily insisting that each type of literature be analyzed by asking:

- Who speaks?

- Who is addressed?

- What is the mood?

Such questions alert one to where, how, and over against whom theological arguments are being made. The setting of Jesus' ministry is one such setting which involved its share of theological confrontation. The writing down of the Gospels a generation or more later reflects a different setting and different kinds of confrontation. The setting of the Pauline letters is clearly a third and much different matter. The fronts being faced were in each case different in decisively important ways.

Obviously, the Old Testament preserves literature that reflects another entirely different series of fronts. The worship of Baal or the dangers of a nationalistic self-confidence are examples of the settings within which extensive theological confrontation took place in the preaching of the prophets. And while the terminology of salvation by grace through faith is naturally missing from these settings, we shall discover later that the underlying prophetic theological perspective and intention in each of those two confrontations find expression in ways which turn out to come amazingly close to the emphases and intentions underlying the Pauline stress on salvation by grace through faith. In order to perceive and examine such parallel theological emphases in different settings, it is vitally necessary to do something more than examine the occurrence and use of the words *grace* and *faith*. It is, after all, possible to deal with the theological concept of salvation by grace through faith without employing those exact words. To listen faithfully to the Old Testament means to allow it to speak on its own terms, and to listen in such a way as to determine what theological affirmations and presuppositions are being made regardless of what theological vocabulary, if any, is being employed.

It is that last point, the possible lack of any theological vocabulary, that constitutes a difficulty of much more prominence in the Old Testament than in the New. Because of the abundance of narrative and legal literature—the vast majority of the Pentateuch—relatively little opportunity occurs for overt theologizing. To be sure, very definite and strong theologies do lie behind both narrative and legal material; they are less explicitly expressed, and therefore less easy to expose and formulate. Nevertheless, the task of investigating grace and faith in the Old Testament is not as difficult as some of the above cautions might suggest. It will actually turn out to be quite easy both to expose and to formulate a very sizable amount of theologizing in the Hebrew Scriptures about grace and faith. It will not, however, be expressed in those words.

In order not to prolong these preliminaries unduly, I offer the following example. To the surprise of many the Book of Deuteronomy turns out to be the most overtly theological book in the Hebrew Bible, and it raises the issue of election, an issue that very quickly brings the question of "by grace alone" to the surface. Because Deuteronomy takes the literary form of a sermon rather than a theological treatise, the listener's ears need to be properly attuned in order to perceive effectively what is being affirmed. Still no one can miss noticing that it is a definite and self-conscious faith that is being confessed here.

When the question arises as to why God chose Israel, the answer is generally given in the negative. "It was not because you were more in number than any other people that the Lord set his love upon you and chose you" (Deut. 7:7a). In fact, the idea of Israel's possible meriting of God's choice because of her impressive size is deliberately rejected by a positive affirmation which is interestingly both beyond investigation and obviously irrelevant: "for you were the fewest of all peoples" (v. 7b).

In later verses another possible motive that might have merited the Lord's choice is raised solely in order to be denied: "not because of your righteousness" (Deut. 9:4-6). In fact, exactly the same kind of reversely-exaggerated and irrelevant claim is also made in this context: "for you are a stubborn people . . . from the day you came out of the land of Egypt, until you came to this place, you have been rebellious" (vv. 6b-7).

However, the Book of Deuteronomy does not confine its reflecting on the reasons for Israel's election to denials of reasons that were not true. It is actually stated why God chose Israel: "It is because the Lord loves you, and is keeping the oath which he swore to your fathers . . ." (Deut. 7:8a). We immediately protest that this is no real answer to the question about God's reason for selecting this people. And we are fully correct in that protest! To say, "He picked us because he loved us," only invites the question, "But what made him love you?" And to continue by claiming, "He picked us because he made a promise to our fathers," is to invite any serious questioner simply to throw up his hands in despair. These are no answers at all. They remind us of a child's smugly irrational way of responding to an adult's, "why" question with an unsatisfactory, "Just because—that's why!"

It really does seem almost that childish. But we should have failed totally in our responsibility of listening effectively, if we left the matter there. True, no answer is given, but the very way in which no answer is given is itself revealing! To answer "Why did the Lord pick us?" by saying, "He picked us because he loved us" is a way of saying that he loves us for his own reasons. He loves us just because he's like that. All our reflection makes it painfully clear that we have nothing that could motivate such love. We are unimpressive in everything but our stubbornness!

This non-systematic way of theologizing is not an isolated example. There is a passage in Exodus 34:6ff. called "the thirteen attributes."[1] In response to Moses' request to see the Lord's glory, the Lord in turn offers to "proclaim my name" to Moses. And in what follows we read: "The Lord . . . proclaimed, 'The Lord, the Lord, a God merciful and gracious, slow to anger, and abounding in steadfast love and faithfulness . . .' " (v. 6). We respond to this list by immediately trying to distinguish between the attributes mentioned. But what is the difference between "merciful" and "gracious"? In fact, there doesn't seem to be any real difference between any of these attributes. The whole list boils down to: mercy, mercy, mercy! What kind of a list is that? Does God have just one attribute? It would appear that this text is saying, "Indeed he does!" And certainly an accurate theological way of summing up all those synonymous attributes of Exodus 34:6ff. would be with the word "grace." Behind the mystery of election there lies only the mystery of what God is like. And the revelation of what he is like—in both Old and New Testaments—comes speedily and unmistakably to center in the word, "grace." And that this is God's one essential attribute is just another way of saying "grace alone."

But there is a further point that needs to be made about the biblical attributes of God. We are more accustomed to thinking of such items as omnipresence and omnipotence as attributes of God than "merciful and gracious." That is because attributes refer to what something *is,* as when a chair is large or soft. Attributes describe the *being* of something. Even though it would be biblical style to say that the Lord *is* merciful and gracious, it ought to be clear that this is a different meaning of "is," and that "merciful and gracious" are different kinds of attributes. "Merciful and gracious" describe God's way of behavior, his actions rather than his being. It is essentially in this way that the entire Bible describes God. In both Old and New Testaments, God's people come to know who the Lord is and what he is like as they reflect on what he has done for them.

It is easy to show the centrality of this action-centered approach to the way God is talked about in both Testaments. To keep it simple let the discussion be limited to brief appositional phrases. Even today a person is often identified by such a brief phrase following his name, for example—Roger Staubach, the quarterback of the Dallas Cowboys. To identify the God of the Old Testament one would say, the Lord "who brought up the people of Israel out of the land of Egypt" (Jer. 23:7). In the New Testament it would be, the Lord "who raised Jesus from the dead" (Rom. 8:11). Fascinatingly, in each case one begins with something this God has done. He is known by what he has done. This is the basic orientation of the theology of both Testaments. Recall that in the classic New Testament summary in Ephesians 2:8, "by grace you have been saved through faith," the word, "grace" functions to describe not God's being but the way he has acted.

Although there is no difference on this score between the approach of the theology of the Old Testament and that of the New Testament, there is still considerable room for divergence within this action-centered orientation. It is possible to identify Baal with such an appositional phrase. One could say Baal, who brings rain, or to quote the ancient texts themselves, Baal, "the rider of the clouds." [2] Notice here that this is not some once-and-for-all act in history, but a continuously recurring act in nature that plays the decisive role as the identifier. Clearly there is a very basic difference in gods that comes to light here.

Baal is a god of nature; in fact, he is nothing more than a part of nature. He is the embodiment or the personification of a part of the meteorological machinery. And, although the seasons continue to change according to their patterns, Baal remains always the same. He is a fertility god. That is his essence. The God of the Bible on the other hand, is known by his acts in history, for this is how he has revealed himself. And history is no cyclically recurring pattern about which one could talk in personification. The essence of the God of the Bible is seen in the way he acts in history. He is gracious and merciful; he has delivered his people.

Essentially, theology is the way we talk about God. God doesn't do theology, we do. And the way Christians do theology is to talk about what God has done. Theology is our response to God's acts. Even the recording and describing of those acts comes as a part of the response to them. Theology is always doxology,[3] because the only appropriate way to talk about God is in response to what he has done—and that calls for praise. This is the way faith finds its expression in both Old and New Testaments. Faith is our grateful response to our gracious God, and praise is the natural form in which this faith is confessed, and in which this gratitude finds expression.

But to understand praise effectively we need to notice its shape. Claus Westermann points out that a teacher wishing to praise a student could conceivably say, "I praise you." But no one would ever say it that way. It would be impossibly stiff and inappropriate. Instead a teacher would probably say, "That was well done!"[4] I prefer the illustration of a young man's words to his sweetheart. Could any lover possibly say to his beloved, "I praise you"? Of course not! Instead the appropriate shape of his praise would be, "You're wonderful!" And that's how it is in the Bible. The shape of faith, the form in which we can expect to encounter faith, is the response of praise on the part of God's people.

To summarize, when we seek to listen carefully to the Old Testament Scriptures as we press our inquiry about grace and faith, we need to be alert to the form in which we can expect to encounter these concepts in the Old Testament. Even though the words grace and faith may not be especially frequent, the realities are there. But we need to be alert because they may come in somewhat different packaging than we are accustomed to. Because theological reflection in the Old Testament comes as the response of praise to God's saving acts in history, we can expect the *shape of grace* to show up as the pattern of God's gracious self-revelation in history. And the *shape of faith* can be expected to show up as the confession of faith by his people in response to that self-revelation.

What is already beginning to become apparent about this matter of shape is that, even though the words may be different, that shape is amazingly similar in both Testaments. No wonder, then, that early Christians should have found it so easy to avow that the God of Israel is the God and Father of Jesus Christ, and no wonder that these Christians should picture the shape of their confession of faith in heaven as singing, "the song of Moses . . . and the song of the Lamb," describing their praise in the words, "Great and wonderful are thy deeds, O Lord God the Almighty" (Rev. 15:3).

In spite of whatever differences our further investigation may show, this much remains unalterably firm—the basic shape or pattern in which we encounter grace and faith in both Testaments is the same.

2

GOD'S GRACIOUS ACTS

THE CONFESSION AND CELEBRATION of God's gracious acts is a major emphasis in the Old Testament. We shall not take the time to explore this aspect in its entirety, for the matters of our special concern show up in the clearest and most emphatic contours in the Bible's accounts of those particular gracious acts which are designated "the wars of the Lord."[5] That grace should be especially at home in the context of war is singularly unpleasant and embarrassing to us. Wars are examples of great evil, so how could they be viewed as the context of God's grace?

The simple fact of the matter is that Israel's existence as a nation was threatened by the attack of enemies virtually from the first moment. In Exodus 17, only a short while after the creation of the nation, Israel was attacked by the Amalekites. Israel fought in its defense, but the whole matter of this kind of war receives a strikingly special kind of treatment in large parts of the Old Testament. Such wars have been given the label, "holy wars," [6] although they differ considerably from either the Crusades or the Muslim wars to extend the territory of Islamic faith. For Israel holy wars, or the wars of the Lord, were those battles in which God gave them the victory. In fact, it was often said, "The Lord fights for them" (Exod. 14:14 and 25).

Generally, some special circumstances of the battle make it plain that God's action is the decisive factor. In the case of the Amalekites in Exodus 17, it is Moses holding up his hands which is the decisive factor, rather than the valor or weapons of the men of Israel. Already Exodus 15 looks back at the exodus as a holy war. The Song of Moses begins: "I will sing to the Lord, for he has triumphed gloriously" (v. 1), and soon thereafter it is proclaimed that "The Lord is a man of war" (v. 3).

This particular area is of such vital significance for our subject that we shall take one individual example and work through it in some detail. Judges 6 and 7 record the familiar story of how, when the Midianites gave the Israelites such a hard time that they were faced with starvation, God raised up Gideon as the deliverer of his people. What I propose to do is to focus on some of the slogans used in this chapter. By slogans I mean those standard formulas that we can recognize as typical from their recurring use elsewhere. By this kind of examination of one example, we can quickly get a picture of what Israel saw as standard aspects of the wars of the Lord.

Gideon describes himself and his attitude in what seem to be strange words, "Pray, Lord, how can I deliver Israel? Behold, my clan is the weakest in Manasseh, and I am the least in my family" (6:15). If we were to celebrate the heroes of our past, "weakest" and "least" would not be adjectives we would choose. Books written to celebrate the victories of the Dallas Cowboys would not describe Roger Staubach as the weakest and the least of the quarterbacks in the National Football League. The only way such descriptions would ever be appropriate for our heroes would be as a way of stressing the great change and improvement they had experienced as they developed into the greatest and the best.

But the story of Gideon maintains its emphasis on the powerlessness of Gideon and Israel all the way through the account. In fact, the development of the story goes out of its way to stress the weakness of the instruments that God used. In the bizarre scene in 7:2-8, two deliberate steps are taken to reduce the number of Gideon's army, and his force is in fact reduced from 32,000 to 300. While we might be tempted to think of this as preparation for praise of those 300, that is clearly not the aim of the account. This is made especially plain by the weird equipment given to Gideon's army: trumpets, empty jars, and torches. The potentially most serious fate that could threaten the Midianites from this ridiculous host would be for an occasional individual in their multitude to be singed by a torch, scratched by a broken jar, or deafened by a trumpet. Bizarre is certainly an appropriate label.

But what we need to notice is the slogan-style language which is used to explain the reason for this bizarre procedure. God is described as objecting to Gideon's large army by saying the people are "too many for me to give the Midianites into their hand." And, as a reason explaining this, the possible danger is portrayed, "Lest Israel vaunt themselves against me, saying, 'My own hand has delivered me'" (7:2). In almost painfully repetitious detail it is made clear that it is God who is the one who gives Israel the victory. Over and over again we hear, "I have given it into your hand" (7:7, 9, 14, 15). The deliberate reduction of Israel's army and the patently ridiculous equipment are simply ways to underline the basic truth intended, that the victory belongs to the Lord. Even the manner in which the actual physical overthrow of the enemy takes place—also a standard part of the holy war pattern—is designed to emphasize the same point. The Midianites are not struck down by Gideon's men, but in panic the enemy soldiers kill one another. As the text puts it, "the Lord set every man's sword against his fellow" (7:22). A divinely induced panic is the means of God's deliverance, with the result that the Israelite soldiers do nothing beyond the mopping up.

In summary, the theology of the wars of the Lord is extremely simple and consistent: God does it all. This is a prominent setting of grace in the Old Testament. In holy war, God does it all. The deliverance of his people comes by grace alone. In fact, just as in the New Testament, great emphasis is devoted to making clear the theological point that deliverance does not come to God's people by what they do, for they do nothing. Truly, a striking parallel to Ephesians 2:8-9, "For by grace you have been saved through faith; and this is not your own doing, it is the gift of God—not because of works, lest any man should boast."

This stress on the God who "does it all" in giving his people victory over their enemies is not confined to the accounts of the wars of the Lord in the historical narratives of the Hebrew Bible. Actually it is in the prophets that this stress receives its maximum development and acquires the role of a basic theological principle. When God's deliverance is promised to his people in the famous "Prince of Peace" passage in Isaiah 9:2-7, the very Gideon episode we have been examining is chosen as an illustration of God's gracious way of freeing his people from their oppressors: "the rod of his oppressor, thou hast broken as on the day of Midian" (v. 4). The point is that the deliverance promised by Isaiah from the Assyrians is going to be like that holy war victory in the days of Gideon. The final line of Isaiah 9:7, "The zeal of the Lord of hosts will do this," is nothing other than the prophet's way of saying, "God will do it all." In Chapters 30 and 31 Isaiah makes the matter crystal clear. In 31:1-3, the faithless people are rebuked for making a treaty with Egypt rather than trusting in their Lord to deliver them. They "trust in chariots. . . . but do not look to the Holy One of Israel" (v. 1). The prophet summons to a different kind of trust. He promises that "the Lord of hosts will come down to fight upon Mount Zion. . . . He will protect and deliver it, he will spare and rescue it" (vv. 4-5). If there were any doubt that this "fighting" of the Lord is of that same traditional holy war pattern, verses 8-9 remove that doubt completely: The Assyrian shall fall by a sword, not of man . . . His officers [shall] desert the standard in panic." Even the typical aspect of the divinely induced panic as the means of victory is picked up by the prophet.

The prophet does develop some standardized terminology of his own, especially in his description of the proper attitude of response by the Lord's people, but we shall return to this a bit later. For now, it is enough to notice that the only kind of war plans of which Isaiah could approve are those that count on God rather than allies for deliverance. In 30:1-3 Isaiah scorns the foolish reliance on Pharaoh by those "who carry out a plan, but not mine; and who make a league, but not of my spirit" v. 1). Carried away by the patterns of power politics, the king and the people are unable to accept the prophetic offer of an "old time" deliverance in holy war style. What such a deliverance would have been like, we hear vividly in Isaiah 17:12-14:

> Ah, the thunder of many peoples,
>   they thunder like the thundering of the sea!
> Ah, the roar of nations,
>   they roar like the roaring of mighty waters!
> The nations roar like the roaring of many waters,
>   but he will rebuke them, and they will flee far away,
> chased like chaff on the mountains before the wind
>   and whirling dust before the storm.
> At evening time, behold, terror!
>   Before morning, they are no more!
> This is the portion of those who despoil us,
>   and the lot of those who plunder us.

In language borrowed from creation mythology the threat of the attacking nations is described as the hostile chaos waters which must flee at the divine rebuke. In a colorful bit of detail the deliverance is portrayed as taking place between midnight and morning. The point seems to be that God's action takes place unobserved. He doesn't want spectators. Recall Lot's wife!

In the later days of Jeremiah, Israel's guilt has gone so far that this prophet transfers the language of holy war from the realm of promise to that of judgment. He speaks of the war trumpet sounding when the Lord himself brings an enemy against Jerusalem. To the consternation of his people who have been deceived by the promises of false prophets, God announces that he is bringing "evil from the north" (4:6), "a nation from afar" (5:15) to destroy his people. And when the false trust of the people and the king moved them—in a time when the hopelessness of all the alliances had become tragically evident —to hope that the Lord might after all deliver them from Nebuchadnezzar, the prophet's reaction is biting and bitter. When inquirers hope that "perhaps the Lord will deal with us according to all his wonderful deeds, and will make him

(Nebuchadnezzar) withdraw from us" (21:2), Jeremiah instead describes the Lord's determination to act in holy war style *against* his people: "I will turn back the weapons of war which are in your hands. . . . I myself will fight against you. . . . I will give Zedekiah . . . and the people in this city . . . into the hand of their enemies" (21:4-7).

When the Babylonian army breaks off the siege of Jerusalem, to drive off an Egyptian threat, the prophet again chooses the language of holy war to announce the folly of his people's hopes. The enemy will return and destroy Jerusalem. In fact, "even if you should defeat the whole army of Chaldeans who are fighting against you, and there remained of them only wounded men, every man in his tent, they would rise up and burn this city with fire" (37:10).

As before, God does it all—only now his gracious deeds have been changed to fierce judgment. But even so the pattern of the past, the pattern of "all his wonderful deeds" (Jer. 21:2), shines through. Although it is now tragically too late, the people have finally learned what is the Lord's way: in holy war he does it all. No matter how small or how weak his instruments, he *gives* the victory as he wills.

The best evidence of all to demonstrate how the setting of holy war has become the way par excellence to set forth God's gracious acts in the Old Testament is the account of the exodus. Although the exodus event far predates the holy wars of Gideon's day, that later perspective had become so traditional as *the* way in which to describe God's gracious act that the language, style, and perspective of holy war are used in Exodus 14 to interpret the underlying meaning of what the Lord did for his people in that decisive deliverance.

In Exodus 14 there is a battle, but Israel does not fight. Instead, just as in the Gideon episode, God does it all. Israel is "only to be still" (v. 14) and "see the salvation of the Lord, which he will work for you" (v. 13). The battle is the Lord's; "The Lord will fight for you" (v. 14). As a result there can be no boasting for Israel over such a victory. The intent of it all is that the Lord "will get glory over Pharaoh and all his host" (vv. 4 and 17-18). Again, as we had noticed in Isaiah's treatment of holy war, the deliverance comes in a manner that the Israelites cannot watch. Israel's first glimpse on that momentous morning was "the Egyptians dead upon the seashore" (v. 30). But they knew full well how to assess the meaning both of what they saw and what they had not seen: "The Lord routed the Egyptians in the midst of the sea" (v. 27). What Israel "saw" without being able to watch anything was "the great work which the Lord did against the Egyptians" (v. 31).

But the theological perspective of holy war is not adequately captured with the recognition that salvation comes by grace alone. This same holy war material, especially in both Isaiah and in Exodus 14, also concerns itself with the character of the response of God's people to these gracious acts. A number of ways are utilized to speak of that response. Sometimes the negative "fear not" (Exod. 14:13) is employed, but it is the positive characterization which concerns us more now. The focus is preeminently on the negative, even when the terminology is at least technically positive. Such expressions as "be still" (Exod. 14:14), "stand still" (1 Sam. 12:7, 16), or "slack off" [7] (Ps. 46:10) manifestly center their intention on what Israel is not to do. Israel is forcefully ordered not to do anything, because that is the only appropriate response to a situation where God does it all.

The word "see" or "look" is occasionally employed, but in a rather special sense, one which seems to border on being a technical term. While Exodus 14:30 and 31 use this word, as has been noted, it is Isaiah who gives us the most striking instances. He employs the word "look" to describe the inner attitude of his people's heart. He denounces them because they "looked to the weapons" (22:8b) but "did not look to him who did it" (22:11b), or "do not look to the Holy One of Israel" (31:1). In this last passage the idea of "looking" is elaborated with some highly illuminating synonyms. "Look" is equivalent to "rely" or "trust." And this turns out upon examination not to be an isolated instance in which the word "trust" is linked up to a holy war situation as the label for the proper response to God by his people.

In Isaiah 30:15 a summary of the prophet's message appears in which both God's offer and Israel's proper response are set forth in programmatic language: "In returning and rest you shall be saved; in quietness and trust shall be your strength." Notice the close connection between the idea of inaction—or "rest" or "quietness"—by Israel, as befitting the occasion in which God does it all, and the idea of trust. In the light of this it should come as no surprise to observe how in the famous holy war promised in Isaiah 7 the prophet gives classic expression to the call for the proper response by God's people in the word-play,[8] "If you will not believe, surely you shall not be established" (v. 9b).

Once again, the accompanying vocabulary leaves no doubt as to what kind of situation is going on. It is a holy war deliverance which the prophet promises. In Judah's fright over the threat of the coalition between Syria and the Northern Kingdom the word is crystal clear. "Be quiet" and "do not fear" (v. 4) are nothing other than the familiar terminology we encountered above. And what Israel is called to do is simply to "believe"—and nothing else. In other words she is called to "faith alone!" Perhaps now we can return with sharper eyes to the final verse of Exodus 14: "The people . . . believed in the Lord!"

Although it may be hard for some with preconceived notions of what can or cannot be found in the Old Testament to admit it, the Old Testament knows full well that salvation is both "by grace alone" and "through faith alone." In fact, it should be fully apparent that this heavy stress on how God does it all, and the nature of his people's proper response as the trusting surrender which simply allows him to do it all, is to be seen as one of the major roots of Paul's theology. As a faithful student of the Hebrew Scriptures he turned to that literature for help in grasping and formulating what he had experienced. I think it is obvious that he found the way God in Christ had acted with him and with his Gentile converts corresponded exactly to the pattern of God's action in those Old Testament deliverances we have examined.

Paul became the theologian of "by grace through faith," not in opposition to the Old Testament, but precisely by utilizing and proclaiming the message of those Scriptures. I'm sure this didn't surprise Paul, for it is fully consistent with his emphasis elsewhere that God's action in the New Testament revealed the consistency of his nature. No wonder he argues that already Abraham was saved "by grace through faith."

Of course, Paul's theologizing had its function within a different setting. For him "by grace through faith" was a slogan rooted in a polemical context. That is, the situation in which Paul's formulation was born was one of confrontation with the Judaizers and their stress on the "works of the law." The holy war theology of the Old Testament did not have such a sharp confrontational orientation as its root. Such a polemical dimension came easily to the fore in later situations, but the original emphasis was much more a matter of celebration than confrontation. Isaiah used holy war slogans to combat the desire by the king and his advisers to build the nation's security on a foundation of military alliances, but at its basis the Old Testament message of the way God does it all is much less a matter of argument than it is one of doxology.

Although there is a clear hortatory dimension in Exodus 14:13, where the people are admonished, "Fear not, stand firm, and see the salvation of the Lord, which he will work for you today," this is not the major emphasis. This is proved by the way no alternative option is fought against. Whereas the king and his counselors in Isaiah's day followed what they regarded as a better founded and more viable choice, the alternative at the shore of the Sea of Reeds was only surrender and disaster. When the climactic point is made in Exodus 14:30-31, "Thus the Lord saved Israel that day . . . and they believed," there is no argumentative adding up of the evidence to clinch a case, no concluding line like the Apostle Paul's "For we hold that a man is justified by faith apart from the works of law" (Rom. 3:28). Instead, what follows is only praise, i.e., the Song of Moses in Exodus 15. But nonetheless, the content of that song is every bit as much an affirmation of the grace of God by which alone his people are saved as anything Paul ever wrote.

The focus in Exodus 15 is, like the Easter message of the New Testament, centered on the mighty act of God, the amazing demonstration of his victorious power: "He has triumphed gloriously" (vv. 1 and 21) and "thou overthrowest thy adversaries" (v. 7). It seems to me the analogy is both clear and convincing. The Old Testament message of God's gracious, saving acts is, like that of the Gospel message of the Easter victory, an affirmation of God's grace. In this the central aspect of each Testament is alike.

However, when need arose subsequently to combat a false

theological approach, this central affirmation had within it the potential to serve as the undergirding of an attack by God's spokesman on that false theology. Isaiah's call to trust in God rather than alliances, important though it is, is not as central to Israel's faith as was the message of the exodus. The saving act of God is the foundational center, while the call to trust only in that God is a secondary step—virtually essential to be sure, and even implicit in the confession of the deliverance from Egypt, but still a second step, only possible *after* the first and foundational affirmation.

Similarly, the Pauline message of justification by grace through faith, important though it is, is not as central to the Christian faith as is the message of Jesus' resurrection. That God raised Jesus from the dead is the foundational center of New Testament faith, while the call to put our trust solely in that God, rather than in any works of our own, is again a second step. Certainly this second step is essential and genuinely implicit in the Easter message, but it is still a second step, only possible on the *basis* of the first and foundational affirmation.

Is not this amazing? Where some have claimed the Old Testament to be a message in contrast [9] to the gospel of salvation by grace through faith, our investigation—as yet in its early stages—has shown the two Testaments to be at one in their affirmation of the primary message of salvation by grace, and even also at one in their affirmation of the secondary explication of that message as meaning salvation by grace alone through faith alone.

3

GOD'S GRACIOUS CHOICES

THIS SURPRISING SIMILARITY between Old and New Testaments continues when we turn to the second setting in which we encounter God's grace in the Old Testament, God's gracious choices. This is an extensive and rather complicated matter, for there are four main choices to which Israel's Scriptures bear witness. Technically they are called election traditions, but in actuality the language used is not technical in that it does not employ abstractions. Instead, some very concrete language is used, for example, "covenant." Literally, a covenant is just a solemn agreement, and the whole usage of this word is nothing but a metaphor borrowed from law, especially international law. Still, even concrete words develop standard formulas in which they appear repeatedly.

The covenant idea is a good case in point, for scholars have noticed how Israel typically expressed her covenant relationship with God without in fact using the word "covenant" at all. The pair of phrases, "I am the Lord your God, and you are my people," has come to be known as the covenant formula, because in it the meaning of what Israel understood by covenant is brought out. As far as that formula sounds, the relationship is a mutual one, but as a matter of fact the mutuality was subject to a strong limitation. It was the Lord who chose Israel and not the other way around. When one inquires as to where that choice was made, there open up two possible answers, which constitute the first two election traditions.

1. MY PEOPLE AT SINAI

According to the simpler of the two traditions it was at Sinai that Israel became the people of the Lord. Of course, God called Israel as his people already back in Egypt, but the covenant at Mt. Sinai was the spelling out or formulating of what that choice involved. The emphasis of the Sinai material is overwhelmingly clear, it was God's gracious choice in which Israel's peoplehood was rooted. As we have already seen in Deuteronomy, it was God's undeserved choice which was basic. Any possibility of merit on Israel's part is carefully rejected. Once again, it is a matter of grace alone, a totally one-sided matter. But the covenant formula—I am the Lord your God, and you are my people—is just as plainly a two-sided matter.

Here we need to proceed carefully for the words we choose to describe this relationship between God and his people will prove to be of the highest importance in our assessment of what kind of theology is involved here. I propose that we label the two halves of the covenant formula as expressions of claim and response. By so doing we do justice to the fundamental biblical emphasis on God's initiative in choosing Israel as his people. There is indeed a second half to the covenant formula, but it expresses not Israel's choice, but Israel's response to being chosen, the obligation that results from being selected as the people of the Lord.

That this is true shows, I think, convincingly in the way the basic deposit of Sinai tradition, the Ten Commandments, is formulated. It begins with the Lord introducing himself,[10] using the first half of the covenant formula, "I am the Lord your God." Then, after the historical qualifier we noticed before as typical biblical style, the focus shifts totally to what Israel is to do. At first glance one could conceivably think the preconditions underlying the covenant for each side were being spelled out. However, a closer inspection makes evident that such is not the case. God has already made his choice, and what is spelled out in the Ten Commandments is not what Israel had to do *in order to become* the people of God, but what she was obligated to do *as* the people of God.

The idea that Israel had to carry out some actions in order to qualify to become the people of the Lord is totally foreign to the whole Old Testament. The whole matter is not one of achievement, but one of allegiance. The Ten Commandments do have a legal flavor, but the kind of legal flavor involved is not that of the conditions of a contract, but rather the consequences of allegiance. As the Lord's people Israel is to express her peoplehood by living in a way which demonstrates that she belongs to the Lord. That means Israel is called to obedience, but it is vital to perceive that obedience is the result of peoplehood, rather than the other way around.

This is once again apparent in the Sinai setting. At Mt. Sinai, Israel is given her peoplehood before she is asked for obedience. She has not yet had a chance to do anything! Her election comes first, her obedience comes afterwards. Or, to put it in

New Testament language which turns out to be precisely appropriate, she is made the people of the Lord by grace alone.

The response which is asked of Israel is a response to this grace. And since we traditionally describe faith as the response to grace, we could speak here of a confession of faith. Actually, I find it more appropriate to speak of a confession of allegiance. In response to God's gracious choice of her, expressed in his saving act ("who brought you out of the land of Egypt"), Israel confesses the obligations incumbent upon her as the people of the Lord. In essence, to recite these Commandments was a way of saying, "I do belong to the Lord."

The New Testament speaks in a precisely similar way about Christian peoplehood. Our Lord has made us his own, and he wants us to be what we are—to give expression to our belonging. To make it flamboyantly evident that we were not chosen because of our works, Ephesians 1:4 describes how God "chose us in him [Christ] before the foundation of the world." And notice how the same verse continues by spelling out what is to be our response, "that we should be holy and blameless before him" (Eph. 1:4b). The whole context of this passage is aimed at "the praise of his glorious grace" (Eph. 1:6). So it is in the context of the Ten Commandments; obedience is the response of faith to the grace of God. Once again the extremely close resemblance of the two Testaments is striking.

We Lutherans, if I may single out my own denomination, have been so zealous in our defense of the grace of God over against good works or human merit that we have often been embarrassed and uncomfortable with the subject of obedience. There is even the facetious story of the German pastor so zealous for the grace of God that at the end of his life he was able to say that to the glory of God he had never performed one good work. In this way he could be absolutely sure that he did not put his trust in his own meager efforts rather than the powerful grace of God.

Because we are aware that the grace of God isn't all that powerful if it doesn't produce any results in our lives, we are tempted to approach the issue of obedience from a quantitative point of view: How much obedience must we show in order really to be the people of God? To be sure, that question is completely inappropriate, for there is no quantitative aspect to salvation. Our calling to be what we are, the people of God, is a 100% calling. God doesn't give tests where 70% is passing; the Ten Commandments don't present partial standards. Neither Old or New Testaments know anything about part-time membership in the people of God. Still, it has become traditional for us to talk about behavior as "more Christian" and "less Christian," thus suggesting the implication that "Christianity," one's membership in the people of God, was the result of one's obedience. The real reason behind this kind of thinking and speaking is, in my judgment, our hesitance to take seriously the biblical perspective on our peoplehood, namely that it is rooted on God's gracious choice of us to be his in Jesus Christ.

Here is a place where the heritage of the Hebrew Bible can be a tremendous benefit to us. To put it crassly, Jewishness has never been a matter of obedience. Circumcized at eight days of age, a Jewish boy enters thereby into the covenant long before his obedience could be a question. The word used in Jewish circles for circumcision is actually the word "covenant." There couldn't be a better way of stressing that it is God's gracious act that brings a person into his people, rather than any amount of obedience which could enable one to qualify. In Baptism, Christians make exactly that same affirmation, for

Baptism too involves a covenant promise whereby our Lord adopts a child as his own and a new member of his family.

Human nature being what it is, the ancient rabbis faced the same kinds of misunderstanding about the relationship between obedience and peoplehood that we have explored here. However, their approach is much less theoretical and dogmatic, being instead delightfully narrative and lighthearted. In response to the question, "How many commandments must you keep in order to pass the test of God's judgment," the rabbis answered with an obvious twinkle in the eye, "One." They then went on to explain that, although we are delivered solely by God's mercy, if a person never obeyed a single commandment, it would look as though that person was trying *not* to be a member of God's people.[11]

But to show the fantastically bold character of this rabbinic wisdom about the connection between obedience and peoplehood, another story must be alluded to. According to this story, a certain small village in Palestine was in desperate straits because of a drought. The local leaders all knew—like James in the New Testament—that "the prayer of a righteous man has great power in its effects" (James 5:16b), and so they sought for the powerful intercessor they needed. When the prayers of all the village leaders proved ineffectual, they took a typically bureaucratic step and formed a committee to search for someone whose righteousness could deliver them. But the committee's efforts met with no success. No one's prayers helped, and the committee had contacted virtually all the town's citizens.

Finally, there was only one man left, a bathhouse attendant. Naturally, someone whose work brought him into continual contact with human nakedness could scarcely be, the committee assumed, effectively righteous. Nonetheless, in bureaucratic thoroughness, they came to this one remaining man and asked,

"Are you a righteous man?" His response was anything but encouraging, when they heard his reply, "You've got to be kidding!" Still, they persisted, "Think hard; did you ever do anything righteous in your whole life?" After all, the fate of their city was at stake! Willing to cooperate, the bathhouse attendant looked them squarely in the eye and said, "Let me think." (The tongue-in-cheek building of suspense reveals a charming dimension of rabbinic theologizing!) At last he brightened and said, "Oh yes, I think I did a righteous deed once. . . . A woman came here once crying because she was in trouble, and I loaned her some money." And the rain began to fall! As the now rejoicing committee members went happily on their way, they remarked, "We were looking for righteousness, but God showed us mercy." [12]

A people who tell such a story show that they know what makes them God's people. They know that they are the people of the Lord solely because they have been chosen by that Lord, and they know that God's choice roots not in their deserving but in his grace. Of course, the word, "grace" is not a part of their vocabulary, but they have the reality!

To approach the issue of peoplehood from the angle of obedience is, as we have seen, backwards. Being the people of the Lord calls not for measured obedience, but for unmeasured rejoicing. To belong to the Lord is both a responsibility and a privilege, but the privilege far outweighs the responsibility. The way peoplehood was experienced in the Old Testament is shown very powerfully in the literature produced at a time when that peoplehood was felt to have been lost, when forsakenness was the dominant mood. In the literature of such times no other dimension of suffering can compare with the feeling of having been put aside by God. Exiled from their land, the promised land, Jews found it hard to "sing the Lord's song in a foreign land" (Ps. 137:4). Nevertheless, the very next line of that psalm expresses a powerful oath never to forget their heritage. And their prophet can offer his exiled people no greater comfort than when he tells how God rejects their idea of having been divorced or put away: "Where is your mother's bill of divorce?" (Isa. 50:1) and then cites the Lord's promise, "For a brief moment I forsook you, but with great compassion I will gather you" (Isa. 54:7). To be the people of the Lord did demand obedience as a response and did involve commandments, a matter to which we shall have to return later, but all this was never perceived as a burden. To be the people of God was viewed by Israel of old in only one way, as the great expression of his grace.

2. OUR FATHERS

But the Bible has other ways of talking about the circumstances of God's choosing his people. According to Genesis and Deuteronomy, God chose his people already in Abraham. In manifest analogy to the covenant at Sinai, Genesis speaks of a covenant already with Abraham, one which was subsequently renewed with Isaac and Jacob. As a part of that covenant, promises are made about the people who are to be Abraham's descendants, and Jacob's name is then changed to Israel to make it explicit that the patriarch Jacob is already himself the nation of Israel in essence. Thus the label "sons of Israel" can and does refer equally to Jacob's twelve sons and to the nation that developed out of this family.

But the particular aspect of this tradition about the election of the patriarchs that attracts our concern here is the character of God's choosing. Once again, the narratives make it dramatically evident that God chooses out of pure grace. The account in Genesis 12:1-3 indicates absolutely nothing about Abraham which could have motivated the Lord's choice. There are indeed powerful reasons for God's action, but these lie not in Abraham, but in the plight of the whole human race. Genesis 2-11 has traced eloquently the disastrous descent of God's good world into the realm of the "curse," [13] and now Genesis 12:1-3 moves dramatically to promise the manifold blessing through Abraham by which that curse will be overcome.

As the narrative unfolds, a three-fold promise is traced: the nation, the land, and the blessing. Yet as the story develops, it looks as though the Lord has made a highly inappropriate choice. In particular, Jacob is vividly portrayed as a devious manipulator, one who certainly deserves not to be chosen. He lies, cheats, deceives and gives ample evidence of being anything but the ideal person for God's purposes. Whatever other purposes these complex stories about Jacob may have, one of their major intentions is to show that Jacob was chosen by grace alone! It is as though the biblical narrator could look ahead at all the future generations of the people of God including our own and, seeing the mass of sin that has always characterized the Lord's rebellious people, reassure us that from the beginning God's choice has been one of pure grace.

As a matter of fact, the narrator actually goes considerably further than this, for, like Isaiah was to do with the holy war dimension of God's grace, he too gives special attention to the response of those chosen by God. And he does this in a way that deliberately highlights the element of faith. In the portrayal of Abraham's response to God, this element of faith is set forth according to such a plainly developing pattern that it seems that this pattern is being viewed as typical, a kind of model for all subsequent generations. The way this development of faith is unfolded is by means of the lengthy delay in the fulfillment of the promise given to Abraham. As a result of this delay, a tension develops between promise and fulfillment, and the narrative itself describes this tension by using the word "believe."

While Abraham begins his response to God's promise by leaving his own land and family, his actions after his arrival in Canaan are far from models of trusting faith. His response upon arrival and discovering that "there was a famine in the land" (12:10), was to leave the land—hardly the evidence of a faith that affirms the Lord's promise that this is to be his land! His reaction to the build-up of strife with Lot is similarly one that seems simply to ignore the Lord's promise. He offers Lot his choice of territory. That Lot chose the Jordan valley and Sodom and Gomorrah so that Abraham wound up with the land of Canaan can indeed be seen as the Lord's over-ruling providence, but it can scarcely be regarded as an expression of Abraham's faith. Suppose Lot had chosen otherwise! Abraham in reality does seem actually to ignore God's promise—a response that can only be called unbelief!

In Genesis 15 and 16, Abraham takes the Lord's promise of an heir with considerably greater seriousness. However, in view of his continuing childlessness, he begins to consider some secondary possibilities. In Chapter 15 he mentions the eventuality that a slave born in his house will be his heir (v. 3). When God rejects this alternative and reaffirms instead the promise of descendants born to Abraham, a further and more complicated alternative is explored in Chapter 16. There Abraham has a child by Hagar, Sarah's maid. One could evaluate this response by Abraham together with the one from Chapter 15 as an instance of half-faith. The promise is taken seriously, but its delay occasions attempts by the recipient of the promise to help matters along.

The outcome of the Hagar episode in Genesis 16 illustrates

how half-faith more often results in trouble and confusion than in fulfillment. Nonetheless the history of Abraham's growth in faith is traced considerably further, the climactic instance coming after the birth of the long-awaited son of the promise, Isaac. In Genesis 22 Abraham receives the totally bewildering command to offer Isaac as a burnt offering. With extreme power and narrative skill Abraham's response here is shown to be one of full faith. He obeys the bewildering order and even verbalizes his as he answers his questioning son, "God will provide" (22:8). In this chapter God evaluates Abraham's response as being one which demonstrates his "fear" of God (v. 12), an Old Testament usage which encompasses both trust and obedience.[14] However, in a summary statement back in Genesis 15 Abraham's accepting response of the Lord's promise is directly labeled "faith" in the famous observation, "He believed the Lord, and he reckoned it to him as righteousness" (v. 6).

As we should naturally expect, the Apostle Paul uses this verse in both Romans 4 and Galatians 3 to undergird his argument about how salvation is by grace through faith. But what exactly happens in Paul's use of this passage? Is it a case like his use of Habakkuk 2:4 in Romans 1:17—taking a passage and skillfully reinterpreting it so that it yields evidence for a conclusion not originally intended? No, the case of Paul's use of Genesis 15:6 is different. His use of "justified" or "declared righteous" actually picks up an aspect of the original meaning of "reckoned." Most likely the usage in Genesis reflects the background of a "declaratory verdict" by a priest,[15] a matter to which we shall return somewhat later. Thus, in reality here, Paul has once again used Old Testament language because it fit. He has not only recognized that the portrayal of faith in his Hebrew Bible is similar to what has been his own experience; I would contend that it was his study of this Old Testament material that helped to provide both the shape and the terminology of his famous affirmations about justification by grace through faith.

Even more of the New Testament message of salvation turns out to reflect and even to have been influenced by the narratives about the patriarchs. The Joseph story traces the further advance of the people God chose, but stands in sharp contrast to the preceding stories about Abraham, Isaac and Jacob. Instead of a series of virtually independent accounts as the stories about the earlier patriarchs are, the Joseph story gives ample evidence of being a connected series of episodes, all integrated into a complex plot. The Lord, however, seems almost completely hidden in the whirling complications of disaster and near disaster, guilt and punishment. It is precisely this characteristic, the seeming hiddenness of God in the happenings which befall Joseph and his brothers, that constitutes the underlying unity by which everything is held together in this story. So much of what happens seems so natural: sibling rivalry, revenge, famine, and international politics, that only the reader who already knows the outcome can appreciate what is really being recorded.

The future progress of the story is continually endangered. If the brothers had decided to kill Joseph, if Potiphar had taken the more natural step of having the slave accused by his wife put to death, if a butler's bad memory had not revived at just the right moment—if any of these crucial elements of the plot had not worked out in exactly the proper way, then—then what? It is not a matter of the fate of Joseph that occupies this narrative; the subject is the fate of the whole nation of Israel. As Joseph himself reveals at the story's end, in words spoken to his brothers: "You meant evil against me; but God meant it for good, to bring it about that many people should be kept alive" (Gen. 50:20).

Here is an amazing witness to how the Lord exercised an absolutely total and continuous control of the events of individuals, nations, and international agriculture—and all in a completely hidden way, forcing no one to do anything other than what that person willingly intended. Most overwhelming of all, as Joseph's words point out, is the way human evil is also incorporated with sovereign ease into God's plan. The great saving act of God in the Old Testament, the exodus of his people from Egypt, was made possible only through God's utilization of human evil for the carrying out of his gracious purpose. Exactly in the same way, the New Testament writers bear witness to God's hidden way in the cross. The great saving act of God in the New Testament happens through the deliberate evil actions of men who are doing just what they choose to do. They act in full freedom, but with the same sovereign ease the Lord through their evil brings about the greatest good, that his people should be delivered.

Not just Paul, but the apostolic preaching in general sees in this amazing hidden control of history the climactic revelation of the grace of God. The extreme and even barbarous rejection of the Christ of God by the people of God is confessed as the praise of sovereign grace: "you denied the Holy and Righteous One, and asked for a murderer to be granted to you, and killed the Author of life, whom God raised from the dead" (Acts 3:14-15). This gospel of the cross, which is folly to both Jews and Greeks, must be affirmed as "the wisdom of God . . . wiser . . . and stronger than men" (1 Cor. 1:23-25).

This stress on the hiddenness of God is exposed to a whole host of dangers. That God hides himself may or may not be good news; it all depends on what it is about God that is hidden. Here there is no malevolent "gotcha!", here there is only triumphant grace, the carrying out of the promise made to the fathers.

In a world everywhere exhibiting the power of the curse, God chooses one man's family as the vehicle for a blessing for all the families of the earth. And that he brings this fantastic plan to fruition calls for a particular kind of response. This story cries out to be told and retold out of the conviction that what has happened here makes all the difference for all the world. And as we all know, the name for that conviction is faith.

3. DAVID

What we have seen so far should be enough to make amply clear the link between grace and faith as seen in the Old Testament and those same two realities in the New. But there is more—not because there is need for it for the sake of argument, but just because it is there. It is there in the biblical witness, and, therefore, it belongs here in our investigation. For example, there is David.

The God who is described as choosing Israel in a covenant established at Mt. Sinai, and who is likewise pictured as choosing Abraham, Isaac, and Jacob by a covenant, is also portrayed as choosing David and making a covenant with him. The way this last choice takes place is considerably different from the preceding ones and deserves a close look. David is actually chosen as a replacement for Saul, whom God had chosen and then rejected. The beginning of the story of David is deliberately tied to the end of the story of Saul. At the end of 1 Samuel 15 it is observed that "the Lord repented that he had made Saul king" (v. 35b).

The idea of the Lord's repenting, that is feeling sorry that he had done something, is a bold application of human feelings to God, but it is not uncommon in the Hebrew Scriptures. However, the usual way in which this notion appears is in a description of how God felt sorry about some punishment he had sent upon his people. Out of his sorrow he changes his mind and takes away the punishment. The idea of God changing his mind like that is a good deal more casual than many people find comfortable as a way of talking about God, but at least the whole pattern of behavior is reasonably clear. What makes the passage in 1 Samuel 15 especially unusual is that it is one of the only two passages in the whole Old Testament in which God is described as repenting of doing something good for his people.[16] The other time is described in Genesis 6:6. There "the Lord was sorry that he had made man on the earth." It was God's seeing the great wickedness of his creation that prompted this regret on his part. Still, God's sorrow over his rebellious creatures and his decision to destroy this creation through a flood is only the prelude to a new and unbreakable promise described in Genesis 9:11-12. There God establishes his promise in the form of an inviolable covenant that "never again shall there be a flood to destroy the earth." Thus, God's changing his mind about something good he had done—sharp language though it may be—is actually the first step toward his doing something better.

It is exactly that same way with God changing his mind about Saul. 1 Samuel 15 ends with God's grief over having chosen Saul, and Chapter 16 begins by describing how instead he chose David. Interesting as an incidental underlining of the gracious character of God's choices is the way David was chosen. He was the last of his father's sons. In a culture that gives preference to the first-born, David was a far from likely choice. He was "the runt of the litter." How unlikely a choice David was is further shown in the account by the fact that he is not even present with his father and brothers, but is out keeping the sheep.

Still, as the narrative itself points out, "the Lord sees not as man sees" (v. 7). God picks the last and the least, just as he had done with Gideon. He does it that way to magnify his grace. And God's choice of David is even described—in parallel to the promise of Genesis 9—as an eternal, unbreakable covenant. In 2 Samuel 7:15 the contrast is expressed in so many words. "I will not take my steadfast love from him [David], as I took it from Saul." And in 2 Samuel 23:5 David speaks of how God "has made with me an everlasting covenant." In Jeremiah 33 this covenant with David is compared for its certainty with God's unbreakable covenant with the day and the night (vv. 20-21).

The reason this covenant of God with David received all this reiterating was because it was not just a covenant with one man. God's commitment was not just to an individual, but to a family. God's choice of David's family was the root promise on which all of Israel's messianic hopes were based. The promise that an anointed king from David's line would sit forever on David's throne as king over the people of the Lord is the basis on which the Davidic dynasty existed for over four centuries. This is clearly shown by the way Psalm 89, especially in verses 19-37, ties back up to the account of this promise in 2 Samuel 7:1-17. And it is the hope for an ideal king from this line which is developed by the prophets into the expectation of an ultimate ruler and deliverer of God's people.

But what concerns us particularly here is the gracious way in which God's choice and promise are made. In the passage in 2 Samuel 7 describing how this electing promise came about the major aspect emphasized is that of the Lord's unexpected and undeserved grace. The account begins with David's intention to build a house or temple for the God of Israel, but this offer is declined by the Lord. Instead, by a charming play on words, the Lord declares his intention to build the house, or dynasty, of David. Absolutely no motivating factor is provided for this promise other than the Lord's decision. David's interest in temple building is not viewed as something to be rewarded. It is instead rejected as mistaken and out of harmony with Israel's history.

In view of the distaste with which so much of the Old Testament viewed Saul and the beginning of a monarchy in Israel, it can only be noted with amazement how 2 Samuel 7 commits the Lord of Israel not merely to one man as king, but to this man's descendants forever. As traced above, the contrast with Saul is deliberately underlined, not to magnify any difference in character between Saul and David, for nothing along this line is even hinted at, but to magnify God's grace. David's prayer of praise to God who has done "all this greatness" is just another way of saying that very thing. And David's prayer singles out especially the way this promise commits the Lord to unseen futures, to whatever this dynasty may turn out to be. The promise expresses no unrealistic hopes about the behavior of David's heirs. Instead, their sin is openly anticipated as it is clearly announced "When he commits iniquity, I will chasten him" (v. 14).

But it is left for the subsequent chapters to trace how drastic a role sin was to play in the carrying out of this promise about the Davidic dynasty. The remaining chapters of 2 Samuel trace the first fulfillment of this promise through Nathan that after David one of his sons would rule on his throne. This justly famous succession history follows the affairs of David's household with an unflinching frankness unmatched in the ancient world. Out of the welter of potential heirs seeking

David's throne the narrative follows the path that leads to Solomon as David's successor. And what a path it is! It begins with adultery and murder, for so Bathsheba, the mother of Solomon, is brought on the scene. Political plots, rape, murder, and revolution are a few of the steps along the way. And yet through it all—as in the Joseph story—the hidden hand of God is in total control in spite of the way evil people freely determine and carry out their vicious plans.

Make no mistake about it, this narrative does not trace the path by which God "adjusted" his choice to the way things worked out. Quite the opposite, even the tiniest seemingly accidental details are carefully woven into the pattern of the Lord's continuous, hidden control.[17] The pattern is one of guilt and punishment, but it is also one in which God's using of human evil to further his gracious promise is attested with a boldness matched only in the account of the crucifixion. The God who condemns David's sin to receive truly fitting punishment in the violence and sexual turmoil within his own family, also grants Bathsheba a son, and the narrator takes the occasion to reveal the whole plot in advance as he observes tersely at the infant's birth, "And the Lord loved him" (2 Sam. 12:24b).

In the following pages Amnon, Absalom, and Adonijah are all eliminated in a swamp of intrigue and violence. But in it all God's hidden purpose moves with resolute ease toward its fulfillment: "the Lord had ordained. . . ." (2 Sam. 17:14b). Even the final events in Solomon's path to power are not seen as lifted above these murky depths of power-hungry intrigue. It is by a harem conspiracy and with a bloodbath in which his opposition and potential rivals are eliminated that Solomon's kingdom is finally established. But all this stress on sinful human plotting in no way deters the writer from his point. This is the first fulfillment of the Nathan promise, and—as one of Solomon's rivals observes about the kingdom's coming into Solomon's hand—"it was his from the Lord" (1 Kings 2:15). The God who is so keenly aware of the evil in the hearts of his followers knows full well that there is only one way he can work through these people, and that is by grace alone.

The succession history does not express itself in any overt kind of response to this amazing path taken by God's promise. The story's blunt confession of God's power secretly at work in the midst of human evil is itself eloquent praise and a fantastic affirmation of faith. Simply to recite what God has done is to confess faith. David's prayer in 2 Samuel 7:18ff. takes this tack and sets the tone for all that follows. He confesses, "There is none like thee" (v. 22), and he goes on to affirm the saving acts of old in which God chose and redeemed his people by doing "great and terrible" things (v. 23).

But the events that follow in the family of David whose family God chose are no less "great and terrible." They are in fact so terrible that we shudder as we trace them, recognizing how similar this pattern of human evil and sovereign grace is to what we see at work in our own lives. The only words that give effective expression to the faith that stands marvelling before God's triumphant hidden grace are words from a much later and yet essentially identical confession of faith. "O the depth of the riches and wisdom and knowledge of God! How unsearchable are his judgments and how inscrutable his ways" (Rom. 11:33).

4. JERUSALEM

There is yet one more election tradition to consider; God chose Jerusalem. For people who are not citizens of the Middle East, there is a strong element of romantic symbolism involved in the very name Jerusalem. The day I wrote these lines, I was shown a newspaper ad that offered a sample of "the holy soil of Jerusalem" in "beautifully colored vinyl" for $6.95 postpaid. To the microscope, Jerusalem's dirt is no different than that of any place else, but that someone could see it as special demands that we try to understand the perspective from which this "specialness" could be affirmed. The perspective of the newspaper ad was nothing but pious foolishness.

However, a number of psalms speak of Jerusalem in a way that reveals an approach in some measure similar to that of the newspaper ad. Psalm 48 regards Jerusalem as "the joy of all the earth" and "beautiful in elevation" (v. 2). The objective observer will note that Jerusalem is not as lofty in elevation as several nearby hills and that it is scarcely the sort of place to which the National Park Service would be attracted for its natural beauty. In spite of that, the psalm does provide us with a key to understanding both the why and the how of the Old Testament perspective toward Jerusalem. That psalm begins by identifying Jerusalem as "the city of our God" (v. 1). By virtue of its being chosen as the site for God's house, the temple, Jerusalem has become the holy city, that is, the city that belongs to God. The presence and the promise of the Lord are what make Jerusalem special, and the physical characteristics of her appearance are drawn into her specialness as a way of describing her invisible glory by means of what can be seen.

The Old Testament celebration of the glory of Jerusalem in the description of her physical beauty is nothing other than a way of pulling back the veil that blocks off as invisible the true glory of this city chosen by Israel's God. And even the language of Psalm 48, particularly such a line as "in the far north" (v. 2), gives away the means by which this celebration of the hidden glory of the city of God takes place. Jerusalem was, of course, not in the far north—either of Palestine or of anything! But the psalm borrows the imagery used by Canaanites for whom the mountain of the gods was indeed situated in the far north. We might paraphrase and call Jerusalem, "the real Olympus." Indeed such imagery is not to be taken literally, but neither is it to be dismissed as insignificant. The only way to understand such enthusiastic celebration of Jerusalem is in the light of the real root of its significance for the people of the Lord, the history out of which came the temple and the promises of God linked to it.

To our spiritualized Western tastes the idea of any specially holy place is offensive. We know that neither on Samaria's Gerizim, nor in Jerusalem is the Father to be worshiped, for he is to be worshiped in spirit and in truth. But while we find this idea from the Fourth Gospel adapted to our spiritual palates, we gulp uncomfortably at the scene of the New Jerusalem coming down out of heaven. And yet both perspectives are a part of our heritage. In order to have a nation—and that's what Israel for a large part of its history was—a place is a necessity. We wince at the memory that this place had to be seized from other owners by force and bloodshed, but that is an inescapable part of God's choosing of Jerusalem. So also is the defense of Jerusalem against its attacking enemies throughout its history an inescapable part of what God's choice meant. It is especially this military language that we need to examine more closely, for it is within its scope that some vitally important dimensions of the biblical material on grace and faith are to be found.

There is no real narrative recording how and on what occasion the Lord chose Jerusalem.[18] Instead the Jerusalem or Zion traditions in the Old Testament focus on God's promises of protection for the city. The prophetic material reveals how the prophets at times supported and at times rejected the idea of the so-called inviolability of Zion. As we have already seen, especially Isaiah offered God's promise of holy war style protection and deliverance to Jerusalem, only to have King Ahaz reject this offer in favor of a treaty with Assyria. And it was also pointed out how Jeremiah, when he announced God's destruction of Jerusalem, was threatened with death for having assailed a trust in Zion which had evidently become a national dogma since the days of Isaiah.

Psalms 46, 48, and 76 reveal some details about this tradition of the inviolability of Zion. In them we read of the holy war style deliverance by which the Lord graciously delivers his people from the onslaught of hostile nations. The picture of the thundering of nations against God's people in Isaiah 17:12-14 reflects the same kind of assurance. Sadly, this tradition of God's deliverance seems to have developed into a presumptuous "mis-trust" which then in turn called down God's verdict of judgment in the time of Jeremiah.

It is important that we analyze the theological implications of this development. God's promises show his grace, but his cancellation of his promises of protection when he himself raised up enemies to destroy his city demonstrates that God's promises insist on an appropriate response. When this faithful response is not forthcoming, God takes the drastic step of destroying the nation and the city he had chosen. But most important, this destruction was not just the final step in some sort of tragedy; it was also a key step in God's redemption of his people from their own false trust. Since their nationhood had become a barrier to God's purposes through them, God responded by amputating their nationhood and then recreating them as a people that was no longer a nation.

Amazingly in this process God's ancient promises to Zion are not forgotten, set aside or ignored. Rather these same old promises are reinterpreted and given new meaning for a new situation. When Deutero-Isaiah presents the message of the return from exile, Zion, which used to be a geographical label, now becomes a label for the people.[19] And to this people a new and greater promise of protection is later given, "the powers of death shall not prevail against it" (Matt. 16:18).

Other even more surprising transformations take place in connection with the traditional picture of the coming of the nations to Jerusalem. This scene, which is one of threatening onslaught in Psalm 48, is transformed into a peaceful pilgrimage of converts in Isaiah 2:1-4 and even further into a host of gift-bearing worshipers in Isaiah 60:1ff. But fascinatingly even this is not the final stage of reinterpretation. When it is said that "the wealth of the nations shall come to you" in Isaiah 60:5 and 11, this is meant literally, as the contemporary parallel in Haggai 2:7 shows.

The story of the coming of the Magi with their gifts of gold and frankincense follows up exactly what had been promised in Isaiah 60:6, but in the life's work of the Apostle Paul it becomes apparent that the true "wealth of the nations" which comes to Zion is the *people* of the nations who come to the new Zion via conversion as a result of the extension of the gospel to the Gentiles. In retrospect we can only label such a fantastic process of transformation as a triumph of grace, for the transformation in the meaning of these passages is only a reflection of the transformation God wrought in his people as he brought them back from death to life and made the very instrument of their punishment into the means by which their original purpose as the vehicle of blessing for all the families of the earth found realization.

Of course, all along the line the major threat to the fulfillment of Israel's purpose was the response of the people. Where the people of God tried to take over the control of God's promises, as in the assumption that God could not let Jerusalem fall, there the intent of God found frustration rather than realization. Only the faith that responds to God's grace by acknowledging his sovereignty even over his own promises, only that kind of faith is a proper response to grace.

Rather naturally, but nonetheless tragically, the New Testament people of God is heir to the same temptations to "false trust," presumption, and triumphalism. To confuse the promises of God with the desires of our own hearts is nothing other than a self-confident presumption which as always cries out for judgment. And to find Zion's riches in the splendor of cathedrals, statistics, and programs rather than in the opportunity of being the servant of God given to the world is a confusion of values so insidious that it is virtually equivalent to a loss of identity. Apart from its true calling the people of God is simply not the people of God at all.

4

GOD'S GRACIOUS LAW

THE OLD TESTAMENT IS UNANIMOUS in affirming that the central place in which God's grace is to be encountered is in his law. That seems impossible for us to accept in view of what Paul says about the law. And it seems ridiculous for me to mention this point now. If the law is central, then this book should have begun there. Why start out by looking at God's gracious acts and choices, if something else is actually the heart of the matter?

The fact is that we did begin with the law. "Law" is the label for the first five books of the Old Testament. Jews call them the Torah, and that is the word we commonly render as "law." The three parts of the Old Testament canon are: the law, the prophets, and the writings. The whole of this canon can, in fact, be designated "the law." [20] In other words, from the point of view of the Old Testament itself the exodus, the central saving act of God, is a part of the law; it is recorded in the law.

But that surely is not what Christians ordinarily mean with the term "law." Out of the Reformation heritage comes the tradition that law means God's demands and threats. The Lutheran Confessions state that "the law always accuses." [21] And that tradition of usage did not originate with the Reformation. It comes straight from the Apostle Paul.

To the heirs of the Reformation it seems highly surprising that the saving acts of God could be referred to as the law. To use that kind of language must be some kind of misunderstanding, for after all, the labels for the parts of the Old Testament canon are not contained within the Old Testament itself, but are in fact a development of later Jewish tradition. But in the last analysis that line of argument is of no real significance. A good bit of the Old Testament itself does use the term, "law" to refer quite definitely to God's revelation of his grace and not his condemning demand. Psalms 19 and 119 are quite explicit here. "The law of the Lord is perfect, reviving the soul" (Ps. 19:7) and repeatedly "I love thy law" (Ps. 119:97, 113 and 163). And it is not a case where "law" means something totally different from what we have customarily thought, for parallel verses in Psalm 119 speak of loving "commandments" (vv. 47-48 and 127) and "precepts" (v. 159). No, what we have stumbled on here is a matter of great importance and one which must be looked at closely. To refer to God's saving acts as law is not a matter of a weird coincidence or using an inappropriate label. Rather, the Old Testament's own usage will show us that we need to learn anew what "law" really means.

The common, everyday word for law in the Old Testament is this Hebrew word *torah*, which means, "pointing the way." [22] It is commonly associated with what a priest can provide. According to Jeremiah 18:18 and Ezekiel 7:26, one received a "word" from a prophet, "counsel" from a wiseman, and "law" from a priest. There is an incident described in the Book of Haggai which enables us to see this literal meaning quite clearly. In Haggai 2:11, the Lord directs the prophet to "ask the priest to decide this question." What this verse says literally is: "Ask the priests for *torah*." In other words *torah* means "guidance," or "instruction." The reason you ask for guidance, for someone to point out the way to you, is simply to get where you want to go and to stay out of trouble. To show somebody the way is a gracious thing, especially so when there is a real danger of getting lost. God graciously points out to his people the way of life. To live in this world is not an easy matter, and there are indeed real dangers.

In a drastic simplification which goes quickly to the heart of the matter Deuteronomy 30:15 speaks of there being only two ways, one of life and one of death. Jesus in Matthew 7:13-14, picks up that same idea. As a bearer of the tradition about God's will for his people, a priest could be counted on to give guidance along the path of life. This priestly guidance or *torah* came ordinarily in the form of a specific answer to a specific question, but the Book of Deuteronomy as the book of *torah* (Deut. 17:18) was the summing up of all of the guidance God wanted given to his people. The proper theological label for this kind of summing up of God's will is revelation.

That revelation could have various sorts of content. It could be a demand or a threat, but it could also be a promise or a blessing. Deuteronomy clearly sees itself as a gracious revelation, one that is "for your good" (10:13). Deuteronomy is fully aware that this "law" or *torah* is no idle matter: "It is no trifle for you, but it is your life" (32:47). And this revelation does contain God's commandments, but that does not thereby make it a matter of threat or accusation, far from it! Deuteronomy 30:11 observes that "this commandment which I command you this day is not too hard for you." "It is in your mouth and in your heart, so that you can do it" (30:14).

These are hard words for Lutherans to hear. We have come to think of God's law as an impossible demand, one that could only drive a person to despair and would forever accuse one of having failed to fulfill it. Is not that what Paul and Luther said? What is wrong here? Or perhaps we ought to ask, who is wrong here? Is it Paul or Deuteronomy who speaks the truth? Certainly they cannot both be right!

Precisely here many Christians (and perhaps we Lutherans most of all) are the heirs of a great misunderstanding. What many Christians of past generations have done is essentially to begin with a misunderstanding of the Apostle Paul and then go on to twist the Old Testament so that it might fit with this misunderstanding of Paul. Because this whole issue is subject to such great confusion, it is necessary to work through the matter carefully. Paul observed that the law brought death (Rom. 7:10), and that observation is indeed an accurate analysis of what happened in the history of God's people. For Paul, that history culminated in the death of Christ, rejected by that very people whose salvation he brought.[23]

The starting point of the Christian misunderstanding of the law began at just that point, when this Pauline analysis of history—a history that was an integral part of the way in which God's salvation was given to the world—was transformed into an analysis of the life of each individual. Instead of seeing Paul as describing the place of the law in the history of God's saving work with his people, Paul was interpreted as describing the pattern of each individual's life. According to this common interpretation, Paul was viewed as saying that each person's life—his own included—moves from

(1) the prideful attempt to justify oneself before God by a work-righteousness, a meritorious keeping of the commandments, to

(2) the despairing awareness that such self-salvation is im-.possible because our inherent sinfulness prevents us from perfect meritorious obedience, and finally, to

(3) the blessed recognition that all such self-salvation is antigodly folly, for God in Christ has taken away our guilt in his free, saving forgiveness.

Now this pattern is indeed a valid description of the experience of some people—among them Martin Luther—but it does not correspond with the spiritual life of the Apostle Paul, and more important it does not constitute God's intended pattern for every individual. This misunderstanding which sees Romans 7 as both autobiographical and a capsulizing of everyone's spiritual odyssey is the natural result of two underlying reasons.

First, and for followers of Luther, most influential, is the fact that this pattern of a vain attempt to secure God's favor by keeping his commandments was Luther's widely publicized experience, from which in truth he was delivered by his study of the gospel of God's grace as proclaimed by Paul in this very Letter to the Romans. With hearts attuned to Luther's experience, many Christians would naturally assume that the Apostle whose message of "grace alone" became Luther's watchword must have lived through a parallel struggle of his own.

Second, Paul does after all speak in Romans 7 of an "I." What would be more logical than to assume this "I" was an autobiographical one! However, our knowledge of Paul's earlier life within Judaism and most especially his own words about this period in his life in Philippians 3 make it abundantly clear that Paul's life did not in point of fact parallel Luther's. Paul was by his own testimony a good Jew, "as to righteousness under the law blameless" (Phil. 3:6). We hear nowhere from him of any desperate struggle to achieve through obedience a certainty of salvation.

Thus far the whole matter I have called a great misunderstanding could well be nothing more than a question of some purely historical interest, whether Paul's spiritual pilgrimage had been similar to Luther's or not. However, Christianity in general (and perhaps Lutheranism in particular) has often made far more of this issue than a matter of biographical detail in the study of Paul. The Lutheran tradition for example has gone on to generalize on the basis of Luther's experience—and supposedly that of Paul as well—to create a pattern that describes how God works with each individual and even a way of formulating the intention behind God's commandments.

According to this overly ambitious generalization, God holds out to each person an offer of salvation through obedience to the divine law. It is imagined that God had said when giving the commandments, "Keep these and you will thereby become my people; but if you don't obey, if you sin, then I must condemn you to hell!" Naturally, the intent behind this law was solely to lay the groundwork for the gospel, for perfect obedience to God's will is beyond the power of us mortals. And so we Christians traditionally bring the news to the world that Christ has set us free from the guilt that condemns us, and thereby we are also freed from the vain and awful struggle to save ourselves by our own obedience.

Let me make it clear that I in no way dispute that this message is indeed a powerful proclamation of the gospel of God's grace—and even more! This is the only message that can deliver one from the bondage of self-righteousness. However, it must also be pointed out that the role of God's law assumed in this traditional formulation is totally false. Again, it must be made clear that much more is at stake here than some tiny item of historical research. There are two serious and drastic flaws concerning the role of the law assumed in this traditional pattern. The first drastic flaw is that it completely misunderstands the law. The Ten Commandments, which so often (especially in Lutheranism [24]) are seen as a summary of God's demanding will which shows all of us our guilt, were never given as a way of salvation, as a way to become God's people. The law was given, as we saw, to those who by God's grace had already been made his people. To put it plainly and bluntly, the law never was a way of salvation either in the Old Testament or in Judaism.

The second drastic flaw is even more serious. The theology that I have called a traditional pattern actually maligns God's character! What kind of a God would send people to hell for over one thousand years in order to make a point, to make it clear that we cannot earn our way to heaven? If the commandments are to be seen as an offer of salvation available to those who keep them, then this is a false offer. The traditional theology being described affirms unhesitatingly that no one ever did or could earn salvation by obedience. The law is really intended, according to this view, to show us our need of God's gracious forgiveness.

Now, such a theology does not work out so badly when it is one and the same person who is both driven to despair by attempting to earn salvation by works of the law *and* who is set free from this despair by the power of the gospel. Law and gospel as traditionally so labeled have functioned in just this way in many lives.

But what kind of a God is it who reveals to the Jewish people a way of salvation that cannot work, and then lets them fret helplessly for all those years until the coming of the Christ? Surely such a God was a bad God! Grotesquely some Christians have even been willing to affirm exactly that, that the God of the Old Testament was a bad God, and that Jesus rescued us from this bad God. The early heretic Marcion excluded the Old Testament and subjected the New to sweeping revision for just that reason. The orthodox church rejected Marcion's view, not just because it did not square with what the Old Testament was, but even more pointedly because his view did not square with the New Testament message of the Father's love which sent his Son.

On the contrary, as even our brief examination of the law of God has shown us, the law is received with joy by his people, for it is his loving revelation and the demonstration of his grace. It simply reveals to his people how they are to express their response to the great saving acts by which God has made them his own. The Old Testament laws themselves provide clear evidence that they are not intended as a way of salvation by obedience. There is nothing in those laws that specifies how much one must do in order to qualify; they have nothing to do with qualifying. As we have seen, rabbis could raise the question of how many commandments one had to keep to survive the day of judgment, but the answer they gave was, "One!"

The laws are not threatening even when they deal with severe penalties like excommunication and death. Instead their discussion of death penalties is much like that which goes on today. These death penalties for serious offenses are intended to have a deterrent effect, not as a trap to be sprung on the unsuspecting by some malevolent God. God's law for his people is part of his gracious will. It is intended for life, not for death. But it is not given as a way to gain life, but as guidance for those who have already been given life.

Many of the laws, including the Ten Commandments, are so obviously linked to Israel's peoplehood that it is scarcely necessary to advance any arguments to establish that. Laws about not eating pork, or not working on Saturday do not deal with matters of right and wrong in the strict sense at all. Dietary rules and Sabbath regulations are not an expression of what is right or wrong for everyone; they indicate rather what Jews are to do as God's chosen people. Their behavior in these areas is not a matter of intrinsic right or wrong at all. To keep Jewish laws shows only that you are Jewish. It is a matter of belonging, not of right-and-wrong. A Jew who eats ham is not a person who has done something which no good person should do; he is just someone who lives like a non-Jew.

In addition some of the laws force us to go much farther in recognizing that they are not intended to expose guilt, to threaten and to condemn. Laws about expiation, for example, are still laws, but they have what many Christians would call a "gospel" content. Such a law as the one dealing with an unsolved murder in Deuteronomy 21:1-9 is a clear instance of this. The very fact that it was necessary to set up a procedure for dealing with an unsolved murder indicates a different perspective than our criminal law, but even this difference is enlightening. Our modern laws concern themselves only with "subjective guilt," that is guilt that can be linked to a person. If guilt is only "objective," that is, if a corpse indicates some unknown person committed a murder, no judge need be concerned with penalties until a person can be convicted.

For Israel, there was a greater sensitivity to "objective guilt."

God, who abhors violence and bloodshed, will not just ignore the crime of murder simply because it cannot be solved. So that the wrath of God will not fall upon the entire community where such evil occurs, a procedure must be followed in which the innocence of the people is affirmed and by which God is asked to remove this guilt. God's law provides such a ceremony as a gracious way to remove the guilt. The ceremony of expiation in Deuteronomy 21:1-9 is essentially nothing other than a prayer for forgiveness. It could certainly never be considered a "work" of righteousness whereby something meritorious was done, for the people really "do" nothing. In prayer they ask God to act! Any thought of the traditional sort about worrying whether our obedience to God's law was enough to earn his acceptance is totally out of place in the context of expiation.

The same situation applies to the vast majority of legislation about sacrifice. The sacrificial system was a means graciously provided by God for the life of his people; not a way to gain life, but a gracious provision for those whom God has made his own. Even such matters as sin offerings were never seen as any kind of meritorious works. A sin offering is the acknowledgment that one has sinned. The animal's death is a symbolic appeal to the Lord to accept one's confession of guilt and grant the forgiveness he has promised. To perform such a sacrifice is an act of faith that trusts in God's offer; it is in no sense a "work of the law."

Raising the question about the attitude of the sacrifices, we have turned to the issue of faith which always stands closely linked to God's grace. The attitude of the Israelites toward the law in the Old Testament is the strongest evidence that the law is not properly understood unless it is seen as the revelation of God's grace. There is within the Old Testament not the faintest bit of whimpering about the burden of the law. Nowhere do you find the slightest insecurity about having done enough to merit salvation. There is no picturing of God the bookkeeper with his awe-inspiring record of every detail of each person's life being the cause for frantic concern about the sufficiency of our works to earn his verdict of acceptance. Instead, you find essentially only one attitude toward the law, joy—exuberant joy, even embarrassingly exuberant joy. As was pointed out earlier, this comes to the fore especially in psalms dealing with the law, such as 19, 119, and 1, but it is also to be found elsewhere.

To put it bluntly but accurately, the law is always seen as the object of praise. Psalm 19:7ff. lists the attributes of the law: "perfect, reviving the soul"; "sure, making wise the simple"; "right, rejoicing the heart"; "pure, enlightening the eyes"; "clean, enduring for ever"; "true, and righteous altogether"; "more to be desired . . . than gold"; "Sweeter . . . than honey." Surely this rapturous praise does not sound like "the burden of the law!" Psalm 119 contains 176 more verses of the same thing, and Psalm 1 says of the pious Israelite that "his delight is in the law of the Lord" (v. 2). (For Lutherans who accept the authority of both the Scriptures and the Confessions it certainly seems difficult to reconcile this biblical rejoicing in the law with the characterization of the law in the Apology to the Augsburg Confession as that which always accuses.[25])

It almost seems as if the biblical writings deify the law! They apply to the law a language ordinarily reserved for God. In Psalm 119:31 the psalmist "cleaves" to God's testimonies, while in Deuteronomy [26] Israel is called to "cleave" to God. One's "hope" is in God's ordinances (Ps. 119:43), just as elsewhere [27] one "hopes" in the Lord. One "believes" in God's commandments (Ps. 119:66), as elsewhere [28] one "believes" in God. Just as other psalms sing praise to God, 19 and 119 are really singing the praises of the law. And just as other psalms portray the loyal sufferer as trusting in the Lord, 119:92 sees the law as the psalmist's delight and reliance in affliction.

What provides the key by which to understand what is going on in all this speaking of the law as though it were God is the simple fact that the law is a part of God's word—in fact, the *torah* is the first and basic part of the Hebrew Scriptures. Over and over again Psalm 119 uses "word" as a synonym for law.[29] The law is not God and the psalmists do not deify it. It is, though, the central part of God's revelation containing the account of his saving acts, and in praising the law one is plainly offering praise to the God who gave it. To trust in the law is for the psalmist absolutely no different than trusting in God's promises.[30]

But is it not still true that God demands of his people perfect obedience to his will? Clearly that is true. There are scores of commandments that do this, including the Ten Commandments and the great commandment, "you shall love the Lord your God with all your heart, and with all your soul, and with all your might" (Deut. 6:5). And there are scores of laws that call down curses on all those who do not keep these standards.[31] How then can the psalmist in 119:93 say of God's precepts, "by them thou hast given me life"? And this is no isolated verse, for over and over again [32] standards of righteousness are set forth in the form of lists of commandments, and Old Testament people seem to have accepted such standards in blissful simplicity. How could anyone dare to affirm one's own righteousness in such a way as, "Judge me, O Lord, according to my righteousness" (Ps. 7:8)? Is it some self-righteous hypocrisy or some blind and proud delusion that prompts people to speak in this way?

Of course, it is no such thing. Even to pose the question in that way would be to misunderstand what these passages are saying. Obviously, God's commandments call for absolute obedience. It would be grotesque to picture a version of the Ten Commandments that would be less than absolute. Would it ask us not to murder unless someone really deserved it, not to commit adultery except on Tuesdays, not to steal anything unless it was highly desirable? Standards have to be absolute, or else they are ridiculous.

But that is a far cry from claiming perfection! Indeed, and the psalms are liturgical literature, exactly parallel to our own liturgies, in which no one individual makes claims about himself, but in which each of us affirms our total obligation to God. We are called to live in perfect obedience. Any lesser calling, we have seen, becomes silly as soon as it becomes specific. What the psalms present is a liturgical model of the life to which we are called, the life that is right with God. Sometimes it is easy to misunderstand another person's liturgy, especially if the ceremonial setting is foreign. That is the case with Psalm 7 where a person protests his righteousness. Psalm 7 is a model prayer to be used by someone who has been falsely accused of a crime. The word "righteous" is just the Hebrew word for "innocent." [33]

The Old Testament knows no pride and it sets no pattern of hypocritical boasting before us. Its people sinned as we do, but they as we affirmed both a calling to live in full obedience to God's will and a joyous trust in his forgiveness and salvation. This was their faith, and though they spoke of it as trusting in God's law (since they use that label to refer to God's gracious revelation) we could also say they trusted in his gospel!

5

GOD'S GRACIOUS JUDGMENT
AND PROMISES

AT FIRST GLANCE IT MUST SEEM an impossibility to speak of gracious judgment. To apply the adjective "gracious" to something that stands in total contrast to it seems to indicate that one has so thinned out the content of "gracious" that it has no real meaning left. If that is the case, then anything can be labeled "gracious." No, what is sought here is not in any way to "thin out" the meaning of grace, but to examine the intent of God's judgment. To do that we must again seek to let the biblical material speak for itself, and not press it into already familiar molds.

It is plain that God's judgment issues from his wrath, so that ought to settle the matter. Certainly one cannot speak of gracious wrath! And yet it will prove interesting and enlightening to look at just what is the root of God's wrath. Two surprising aspects of God's wrath as presented in the entire Bible, but especially in the Old Testament, are (1) its root in frustrated love and (2) its orientation toward the future.

The Old Testament is strongly insistent that the wrath of God stems from his jealous love, his refusal to share his people with any other god. Because of this specific focus, we must put out of our minds all pictures of wrath in the sense of curses filling the air when a toe is stubbed or a thumb struck with a hammer. God's wrath is related to his love precisely because his love is so possessive.

This awareness that wrath stems from frustrated, jealous love opens the door to grasping the other surprising and distinctive aspect, its orientation toward the future. A wrath aimed at the past exhausts itself in punishing those responsible for one's anger. It is almost exclusively a reaction, that is, the initiative lies with and essentially remains with the person at whom the anger is directed. The God of Israel is described as experiencing this kind of emotion, but his action in response goes much farther. He insists on taking the initiative for himself so that he can change the future.

The emphasis lies on his purpose. His purpose has been frustrated by his people's unfaithfulness and he refuses to allow that to continue. He wills to carry out his purpose, and his wrath is aimed at that end. Since God's purpose is a gracious one, that his people—all people—might belong to him and find in him the true and intended goal for which they were created and redeemed, it seems obvious that God's purposeful wrath has indeed some very close links to his grace. God does not reject his people for failing to measure up to standards of achievement, for we have seen that their place as God's people was not something which could be earned. Instead he rejects them for failure to respond to his grace. He gave them everything, and they rejected him. Because his gracious love is frustrated, he moves to judgment—but it is a purposeful judgment, a gracious one. It is the prophets who deal most extensively with God's gracious judgment, and thus it is to an exploration of this dimension of their message that we must turn.

It is extremely difficult and bitter for us to realize that what the prophets really say is that God's gracious purpose for his people has failed. We find it quite hard to think of failure as something that could happen to God. But this is exactly the vividly human imagery with which the prophets speak. The very opening verses of the first major prophetic book, Isaiah 1:2-3, say this forcefully: "Sons I have reared . . . but they have rebelled. . . . The ox knows its owner . . . but Israel does not know. . . ." It is often forgotten that the Old Testament has a law about what to do with rebellious sons: after the case is proved they are to be stoned (Deut. 21:18-21)! The unavoidable implication of this beginning for the Book of Isaiah is that nothing remains but the stoning. Similarly in Isaiah 5:1-7 God is described as one who loves Israel and who, using the figure of a vineyard, has done absolutely everything for his beloved— only to find no meaningful response. And so the wrathful Lord announces the destruction of his vineyard.

What is shocking about this well-known aspect of the prophetic message is what it says about God! God is portrayed as impotent to achieve his purpose. He loves faithfully and generously, but his people spurn his love and betray him by running off with other lovers. Particularly Hosea, Jeremiah, and Ezekiel make extensive use of this metaphor of sexual love and infidelity, but essentially the entire prophetic message of judgment is making the same embarrassing affirmation: God's promise has come to nothing! His loving purpose has met with frustration—and so he decides to destroy his people. We have to face the fact that we find this imagery offensive. It sounds like losing one's temper and acting contrary to sound judgment; it sounds too human. That we experience this reaction is evidence of the power and skill of the prophetic words, for this is precisely the reaction they intended their audience to have.

But the prophetic message does not stay the same. Each prophet speaks God's word to a different audience at a different time. Isaiah announced God's judgment to come, and so also Jeremiah. But Jeremiah both announced it and lived through it, for the judgment of defeat and exile happened in his lifetime. His preaching in those days just before the doom came, is changed. There is still accusing wrath, but now it no longer leads up regularly to the announcement of a threatened next act of God. Instead often Jeremiah's oracles lead up to no further announcement than the grief of God. And yet that very grief of God is in itself a powerful revelation. Does it not sound familiar to listen to the voice of the Lord grieving over Jerusalem in frustration, "How often would I . . . and you would not" (Luke 13:34)? Do we not have to call this a grace-filled message of judgment?

Yet the prophetic message of judgment is much more radical than we can accept. The way the prophets express that judgment is by proclaiming that God has canceled his promises. Hosea announces to the Israel God had claimed as his own, "You are not my people and I am not your God" (1:8). This is nothing other than the cancellation of the covenant formula itself; it is the language of divorce! Each of the other election traditions gets a similar treatment of cancellation. To Jehoiachin, the last reigning king of David's line, to whom God had promised in 2 Samuel 7 an eternal dynasty, Jeremiah says, "None of his offspring shall succeed in sitting on the throne of David" (22:30). To the Jerusalem God had chosen as his dwelling place, to Zion the city of our God, Jeremiah said, "Behold, I am giving this city into the hand of the king of Babylon" (34:2). We find this offensive; God ought not to make promises and then cancel them. He should be more consistent, there should be greater continuity.

Clearly this prophetic presentation of God's canceling of his promises is a potent instance of talking about God in human language—but then so is everything we say about God. And you have to concede this in the prophets' favor, their message got through to their hearers. Otherwise no one would have bothered to persecute them. But the prophetic preaching does have a full measure of continuity—embarrassingly so. The prophets stress the continuity of sin. Ezekiel brands Jerusalem as a faithless wife, a slut who has gone chasing after every other god or nation who has come along. Jeremiah and Ezekiel both picture her as degenerate, having sunk to the level of an animal in heat panting after any available partner. And yet the Lord continues to care! Instead of abandoning this tramp to her fate he still seeks to win her back, to purify her love. The extremity of this frustrated but enduring love is doubtless that of Hosea 11:8-9, where God is portrayed as on the verge of destroying his unrepentant and perverse people, when suddenly he stops to exclaim, "How can I give you up? . . . My heart recoils within me. . . . I will not execute my fierce anger. . . ." This is truly an amazing picture, one of the justly wrathful God held captive by the bonds of his own love! Surely this is a revelation of grace in judgment.

Still, this gracious character of God's judgment should not obscure for us the absolutely radical nature of this judgment. The prophets themselves realize full well that their hearers, nurtured as they were in the history of God's gracious acts, would tend to miss the extreme sharpness of their message, and so they deliberately chose the harshest formulation imaginable for it. They spoke shockingly of the death of God's people! In doing so they picked up on the old message of two ways, one of life and one of death, from Deuteronomy 30:15-20. The stress up till now had always been on the invitation to life through God's word (Deut. 8:3; 32:47). Now, though, the death alternative receives a startling emphasis. Amos sings a funeral dirge for Israel (5:2), and sees only enough of a remnant to prove that there was once a people (3:12). Isaiah sees only a similarly insignificant handful of survivors (30:17 and 17:6). Jeremiah envisages only two alternatives: surrender and live in exile or stay and die (21:8-10). Ezekiel announces "the end" and employs language borrowed from the carrying out of a death penalty as he cites God as saying, "My eye will not spare, nor will I have pity" (7:9).[34] In a drastic vision in Chapter 9, Ezekiel sees Jerusalem being destroyed by God's messengers, and when he intercedes for his people, he is again given the word of "no pity."

Surely a death sentence like this is so utterly final that it would make no sense to look for any future-directed orientation here. And yet, if we listen with simple honesty to what the prophets proclaim, we must admit that this is exactly what is characteristic of their preaching. They do speak of death—and yet they offer promises. Judgment is only understood rightly when it is seen as a message of death, and the prophetic promises are rightly grasped only when they are heard as offering life out of death. Oh, they are not dealing with the later apocalyptic hope of a general resurrection of the dead in connection with a final judgment and the promise of eternal reward and punishment. No, Ezekiel, who is the most vivid in this regard, makes eloquently clear just what he means in the famous "dry bones" passage in 37:1-14. He speaks of the Judean exiles as being in death, this being actually their own self-assessment (33:10). And he speaks of a return to their land as a national resurrection.

We look back on this message and rejoice over the magnificent dramatic power of this imagery of life out of death, but it should be noted that no one would ever believe such a message in advance. That would be like going to a doctor and being told that he could cure you—but first he'd have to kill you. I am quite sure no one would ever return to such a doctor for a second visit! We marvel that the prophets called to announce such an impossible message did not simply resign on the spot. Even we as we look back dispassionately on this fantastic message must "rub our eyes" spiritually in order to accept the fact that such a bold proclamation was ever made. But made it was and we need to be fully clear about its intent.

As I see it, this life-out-of-death language is not intended solely to magnify the seriousness of the guilty plight of God's people. That is only the first half of its purpose. To stop there would be similar to seeing the cross of Christ as a revelation of human guilt—and stopping there. To speak of a life out of death must be seen as aimed to magnify the "by grace alone" aspect of God's promise! The prophets are telling their people that they need more than help: they need a miracle! The most fitting analogy is that of Christian Baptism. Here too the old nature must die and the new nature rise from the dead (Rom. 6:3-4).

With the use of that word "new" a key element in the prophetic message of hope has been touched on. In recent study of this motif of "new" in contrast to "old" in the prophetic hope it has been made clear that the primary focus is on the parallel with the old election traditions.[35] That is, a new exodus and a new covenant are contrasted with the old, a new David is promised to replace the old, and a new Jerusalem is looked for as being like the old only greater. There is a remarkable consistency in this pattern of a new-old contrast. In some cases there is naturally a higher degree of continuity possible between the old and the new than in others, but it should be amply clear that we do not encounter here merely an accidental use of imagery, but instead a deliberate pattern.

For the prophets it is a way of affirming that there is still power inherent in God's promises—even his old ones. They are miraculously able to speak anew beyond their cancellation. Beyond "not my people" there can come by analogy to the old covenant the promise, "You shall be my people." Beyond "no heir upon David's throne" there can come by analogy to the old oracle of Nathan the promise, "I will set up over them one shepherd, my servant David" (Ezek. 34:23). And beyond "The Lord has forsaken Jerusalem" there can come by further analogy to the old description of the devastation of the temple the promise, "The name of the city henceforth shall be, The Lord is there" (Ezek. 48:35).

On the basis of this insight into the old-new pattern, a host of biblical passages, New Testament as well as Old, open up in meaning. In each case the use of "new" establishes an analogy to the old, but at the same time, the new is in some way better or greater than the old. Isaiah 43:16ff. speaks of a new exodus, like the old, only greater, and calls on the people, "Remember not the former things, nor consider the things of old. Behold I am doing a new thing" (vv. 18-19a). To call upon Israel to forget the exodus from Egypt seems impossible, even blasphemous, but the prophet's point is the extent to which the greater grace before them exceeds that which lay behind them. Similarly in Jeremiah 23:7-8 the affirmation of the God of the exodus is to be replaced by speaking of the God of the restoration.

The best example, though, of this promising of a new and greater grace is the famous new covenant passage in Jeremiah 31:31-34. If we study that passage from the perspective of asking, "What precisely is new about the new covenant?", we find a surprising and overwhelming answer. The new covenant is not new because it involves obedience from the heart as opposed to the letter of the law. That idea is an old one in Israel, abundantly attested in the tradition preserved in the Book of Deuteronomy. And neither does the newness of the new covenant root in the newness of the laws which go with it. There is in this passage in Jeremiah not the faintest hint of any new commandments, or even any thought that there was something wrong with the old ones. Instead, it is plainly stated that the real problem with the old covenant was just that the people broke it. There was a clash of wills between Israel and the Lord, and the only possible solution is a new will for God's people. "I will put my law within them" (v. 33) is the ultimate promise, the ultimate act of God's grace. He will remake his people so that disobedience is no longer possible for them.

But would not such a new creation make us robots? Wouldn't this take away our part in our lives? Let us be clear, this promise speaks of God's ultimate gift to his people. If we are ever to be fully his, that can only happen by his action. This ultimate dimension of our salvation, like all the rest of it, will happen by grace alone! It will happen not by making us robots, but as Jeremiah 31:34 says, by forgiveness. It will not be some stage along the way; it will be the final triumph of God's grace.

When will all these promises of the new gracious acts of God be a reality? In approaching that question it is important to be aware that all these promised items are expressed in images, as varying aspects of a totality, and not as separate stopping points on some sort of divine timetable. It is wrong to look first for a new land, then for a new Jerusalem, and so on. Such an approach is wrong because it will not accept the truth that the future is hidden in God. Not even the prophets or apostles were given a knowledge of "times or seasons which the Father has fixed" (Acts 1:7). Even after his promises have been given, God remains Lord over his plans in a way that inevitably leads to tension for his people. Deutero-Isaiah's glorious promises of the inauguration of the new age with Cyrus' conquest of the Babylonians must have led to bitter disappointment for the returned exiles who never amounted to more than a pipsqueak province and who considered themselves as slaves (Neh. 9:36) and a dead end in God's saving history.

The sovereign freedom inherent in the Lord's grace always means that his people are called to a faith that allows the future to remain in God's hands. That automatically means patience and tension are a built-in part of what faith involves, but it also means an openness to God's next act in history. In the dark days of Israel's position of subservience within the Persian empire following the exile, the Israel which had lost its political independence had to come to terms with the revised nature of its peoplehood. The promises of a new age and a new covenant remained unfulfilled, but these very promises remained the foundation in hope for their existence as the people of God.

With the passing of centuries and no sign of the hoped-for new saving acts of God, the Jews of the intertestamental era faced the need of coming to terms with this new, interim character of their peoplehood. The basis for their existence as God's people had been switched from the past saving acts of God to his future acts, but no mighty acts happened. As a result, in the interim the role of the law, originally having its significance only within a covenant setting, now began to move toward a position of priority over against the covenant. Now becoming a part of this people meant not so much a change in citizenship as a new pattern of behavior.

Since there was no longer an independent Jewish state, becoming a Jew became a matter of adopting Jewish practices. While some scholars have considered this the birth of legalism,[36] I must disagree. "Legalism" properly defined is a relationship with God based on obedience,[37] but Israel always viewed its tie to God as rooted and founded in God's acts and choice of them. Even when in the post-exilic period the law and obedience to it seemed constitutive for being God's people, it must be remembered that all of this was grounded in the future saving acts of God. Any legalism involved was only potential and not actual, for the expectation of that future in which God by a saving act will establish anew the basis for their peoplehood remained fundamental, even though it may have been at times ignored in the press of daily living in a world where God seemed no longer active in history.

Mindful of this understanding of what legalism means, we can now understand exactly what was involved when the strife arose between Paul and the Judaizers. Paul insisted that no obedience to Jewish rulers dare be demanded of Gentile converts as some sort of prerequisite for their becoming part of the people of God. The reason underlying this stress on Paul's part was his understanding that in Christ God's new saving act had happened. The new age had begun and the new basis for peoplehood had been established. To demand any obedience as a prerequisite for the Gentiles to be included among God's people would be to deny the full adequacy of what God had done in Christ. It would mean that there really had been no change, that "Christ had died to no purpose," and it would be to "nullify the grace of God" (Gal. 2:21). In short, to ask for obedience as the basis for a relationship with God when God himself had established such a relationship purely by his own action, would be legalism and a denial that salvation was by grace alone. Thus it is against the Judaizers that Paul fights so fiercely, not against the Old Testament or Judaism. Over against Judaism Paul speaks about fulfillment, but over against Judaizers he speaks about by grace alone and through faith alone rather than by works of the law. And what is fascinating is that in doing this Paul stands squarely in the tradition of the Old Testament. No wonder he feels so free to use that Old Testament to argue for his position!

This last observation about Paul's using the Scriptures of the old covenant to argue in support of the new covenant brings us to face the same question about the place of the Old Testament in Christian faith. All too often Christians have viewed the Old Testament as superceded, and perhaps naturally so since it has been fulfilled. Paul's use of it, though, points us to a deeper understanding. Because the God and Father of Jesus Christ is also the God of the Old Testament, it should be no surprise that his old words—in the Old Testament—continue to find fulfillment, continue to describe him effectively and powerfully, even to his new people. Further, it should also come as no surprise that faith in this gracious Lord still means that his people are called to continue living in the tension between promise and fulfillment.

That tension is of a peculiar sort, due mainly to the powerful nature of God's words and promise. Isaiah 7 with its offer of a holy war deliverance from the danger of the Assyrians is in one way a tragically sad message, for it is an offer which was rejected. When in verse 14 the Lord promised a sign, that a "young woman shall conceive and bear a son, and shall call his name Immanuel," the bitter truth is that God's offer found no response in the heart of King Ahaz. As a result, nothing came of this promise—in the eighth century B.C. Yet the Evangelist affirms in Matthew 1:23 that this old word of God did not fall powerless to the ground, but found a transcendent fulfillment in Bethlehem, a fulfillment which was analogous to but far exceeded the original promise. So it is that God's old words continue with strange power to bear witness to his new acts.

In similar fashion the word about the new covenant in Jeremiah 31 remained unfulfilled. That promise spoke of a time when God's will would be written on the hearts of God's people so that sin would no longer be a problem and teachers would be unnecessary. In the light of the extreme character of that promise, it seems amazing that the writings of the New Testament could dare to assert that it did indeed find fulfillment in Christ.[38] After all, this is truly an ultimate promise, for it describes an ultimate restoration by means of an ultimate transformation. Surely no Christian could dare to claim to have been remade with a transformed will! And yet, of course, we all do affirm this, for we are all new creatures in Christ. But at the same time, the old Adam lives in us and must die daily in repentance. We are new and we are still old. Like the prophetic message, it is a case of being in death and yet having a life out of death. That new life—every part of it, not just the transformed will—is ours only by grace and only through faith.

True, the Old Testament prophets did not use these labels, grace and faith, to describe what they were saying, but the realities themselves were there. The promise was made solely on the basis of God's undeserved goodness—and the word for that is grace. And the promise still depends on God's future saving acts in the consummation of all things in Christ, and thus is ours now only in hope—and the word for that is faith.

6

SUMMARY:
GRACE AND FAITH IN THE
OLD TESTAMENT

IT IS THE AFFIRMATION OF THIS BOOK that the presentation of
the grace of God in the Old Testament and the understanding
of his people's response of faith are essentially similar to the
way the same two realities are described in the New Testament.
The various Old Testament settings in which these two concepts come to the fore have been surveyed and certain key areas
examined in some detail. It was, I hope, obvious that much
more could easily have been presented by way of biblical evidence to support the positions advocated, for only a selection
of samplings has been given.

One danger in the type of format chosen, which explored in
turn the various ways in which Israel experienced and responded to God's grace in its own expression of faith, is that it might
seem that these various ways were somehow separate and isolated areas of Israel's theology. That, of course, is not so, for the

faith of Israel was a single reality. In fact, the theology of the
Old Testament is characterized by an astonishingly high degree of unity in view of the long and complex history reflected
in the literature involved and the diverse groups who have
formulated and preserved these traditions. Actually, the understanding of grace and faith in these Scriptures is among those
elements that reflect the most solid kind of unity. In the remaining pages the attempt will be made to show what are the
most important aspects of that dynamic and continuing unity.

For the entire Old Testament grace is what God is like. Although the forms of the word grace are not all that frequently
used, it is nevertheless true that grace is God's only essential
attribute. "Merciful and gracious" is a pair of synonyms that
occurs in prominent summaries of what Israel's Lord is like in
all three parts of the Hebrew canon.[39] Gracious is what God
showed himself to Moses to be, what in both confession of
guilt and in celebration of praise his people remembered about
him, and in an amazing tour de force it is what Jonah, that
arch example of Israel's failure, knew about his God but tragically refused to share. But most important, gracious is what the
people of God relied on their Lord to continue to be as they
moved in hope through the glories and terrors of their history
toward its elusive fulfillment. Certainly nothing could correspond more closely to that same stress on God's grace in
Christ which characterizes the message of the New Testament,
especially as it finds expression in the writing of the Apostle
Paul from beginning to end.[40]

This central item chosen for preservation in the Old Testament came to expression in a variety of ways. We have looked
at the way the grace of God surfaced in his acts, his choices,
his law, and his judgments and promises. Nowhere, though,
has there come to light any underlying cause or reason which

would explain this grace. The conclusion seems inescapable: there is nothing that underlies God's grace. It is itself the bedrock, that which underlies everything else. In line with the affirmations made in Deuteronomy 7:7 and 9:4, the only way to speak about what lies beneath God's gracious commitment to his people is the negative one of denying any conceivable reason, such as size or righteousness. God's way of dealing with his people is rooted in sheer mystery, in pure grace. Once again, the parallel to the message of the New Testament is striking.

One aspect of several of the metaphors employed to present the message of God's grace in the Old Testament is that of jealous love. That stress intends to accentuate the possessive side of his love, but the first impression this terminology makes on a modern audience is a negative one. Jealousy does not seem to suit a purely gracious love, for it pictures rather a love which is insecure and even destructive—and most likely also shows a sexist perspective in which a wife is viewed as a possession. Most readers are quick to assume that the view of God's gracious love in the Old Testament must as a matter of course have been a sexist one, but the situation is actually more complicated.

It is indisputably true that Israel's social structure throughout Old Testament times reflected a patriarchal culture, but at the same time it is equally clear that many aspects of Israel's society also reflect attitudes that contained the seeds of the transcending of patriarchal limitations. This is especially true of some of the attitudes about love and marriage. In forthright celebration of the duality of the marriage relationship the woman in the Song of Solomon exclaims, "My beloved is mine and I am his" (2:16). Amazingly it is in mutual possession and in mutual surrender that the ideal is seen! Indeed love is seen as possessive, for honestly it is that—but that it is mutually so is a joyful inconsistency of logic which makes the jealously possessive love of God seem suddenly a much more effective metaphor than first imagined.

This duality was indeed characteristic of the love of Israel's Lord, for while no one ever sought to possess his beloved more completely than he, at the same time no one ever gave himself in love more completely than the Holy One of Israel. And while the analogy of married love is only an analogy, it is surely by far the closest analogy to our position as God's people, for we do belong to our Lord, we are his possession. And yet in fantastic condescension he has made himself ours, for he has committed himself to be *our* God. This is, after all, nothing other than a spelling out of what is inherent in the First Commandment. As Luther liked to put it,[41] "I am the Lord your God" is the perfect proclamation of the whole of God's revelation, law and gospel, for all people. To the rebel who renounces God's lordship over his life, the First Commandment comes as sharpest judgment, "Whether you admit it or not, I am the Lord who is sovereign over your life." But also to the despairing sinner, who shamefully confesses having denied his Lord over and over again and thus dares not claim the Lord as his, the First Commandment comes as purest grace, "Because it rests not in your deserving but in my pure grace, I am still the Lord your God." Such a tremendous love is why infidelity can only be seen as shameless folly,[42] and also it is what makes our forgiveness a miracle to marvel over.

It is at just this point that the Old Testament role for faith comes into play, for faith is response to God's grace. Again, though the terminology may not be there explicitly, the actual character of the response to grace is overwhelmingly similar in both the Old and New Testaments. Faith takes the shape of a confession of allegiance. To the God who says, "You belong to me," the proper response is "I belong to you." This is the commitment to which Old Testament faith refers. No tradition ever laid more stress on the calling of God's people to put those words of commitment into deeds, so that the confession of faith might not be a hollow sort of allegiance. But so also no tradition has ever made it clearer that belonging to God is by grace alone, and that belonging to God is prior to and not the result of obedience.

The Old Testament and the subsequent literature of Judaism make it plain that this matter of allegiance has always been difficult and filled with problems, but the problems were never matters of whether one belonged to God or not, for that for Jew and Christian alike was seen to root in God's action. Instead the problems have all come in the area of behavior: What exactly does our allegiance call for? In sharpest contrast to what would seem to be the natural implication of a tradition in which law occupied such a large place, the Old Testament perspective on allegiance has never been static or rigid. Probably as a result of the way the Old Testament traditions have been collected over such a long span of time, there is an inherent recognition that at different times in response to changing fronts the same commitment will of necessity call for changing responses.

In the face of the temptation to Baal worship, with its embodiment of the power of sexuality in the image of the bull, all images could be prohibited. And this prohibition could come to be viewed as a touchstone for testing the strength of Jewish opposition to pagan gods, to the point where throngs of Jews would offer to die willingly in order to stop the bringing into Jerusalem of the eagle-bearing standards of Roman legions. In this instance an awareness of apostasy as a continuing threat motivated strict adherence to the laws in their rabbinic interpretation as being what allegiance demanded.

At another time in the face of severe persecution Israel's authorities could decide that the details of the dietary laws were not matters justifying martyrdom. In the early second century A.D. it could be decided that a Jew might yield rather than die on any point except idolatry, adultery, and murder. Thus great freedom and flexibility has characterized the perspective in Israel as to what the faithful were required to do to maintain the faith.

Similarly, while Christian creeds have multiplied throughout the centuries in order to spell out what Christian faith means, the New Testament rests content with the simple confession of faith, "Jesus is Lord" (1 Cor. 12:3). Once again, it is the matter of the front over against which one's confession of faith is being made that is decisive. Here the line of continuity is strong from Old Testament to New and into the history of both church and synagogue.

In addition to the confession of allegiance, the other basic way in which faith as response shows itself within the Old Testament tradition is in the confessing of praise. Here we encounter firm evidence to support what has been said in this work about grace in judgment. While the reciting of the acts and attributes of God as savior and deliverer is natural, logical, frequent, and easy to understand as being the response of faith to the grace of God, it is a far different matter to recite the praises of the condemning and destroying God. And yet the Old Testament does both of these in powerful style. The psalms we call hymns abound in praise for the God of deliverance, but there is also a strong strand of praise for God which involves accepting his judgment as just. Repeatedly, the Book of Lamentations bring forth lines like "The Lord is in the right" (1:18). Even in the night of persecution and suffering the confession of faith still includes the confession of praise.

It is, in fact, in praise that grace and faith find their most authentic connection. As a part of the way the importance of praise is stressed in the psalms, one of the most tragic aspects of death is seen to be the loss of the opportunity to praise. In bitterest distress in the face of death the psalms ask, "Is thy steadfast love declared in the grave?" (Ps. 88:11). The assumed answer is, "No." The place of the dead is the land of silence; no hymns are heard there. In agonizing summary it can be observed that the difference between life and death is praise. To be deprived of the opportunity to respond in praise to the grace of God is to be cut off from the most central aspect of life. In praise grace and faith are one, and without praise both grace and faith remain frustrated in silence.

In the light of this Old Testament emphasis we can appreciate much more fully what it means when in the New Testament the victory of Jesus transforms death from the place of silence into the place of singing. The most effective way the Easter victory can be proclaimed is to describe heaven as the place of praise, to affirm that forever the mark of the faithful is their participation with the whole company of heaven in celebrating the triumph of God's grace. There grace and faith will be forever united in praise, and there, unlike this study which has reached its end, the most amazing aspect of grace will be that

> When we've been there ten thousand years,
> Bright shining as the sun,
> We've no less days to sing God's praise
> Than when we first begun.

NOTES

1. George Foot Moore, *Judaism* (Cambridge, 1950) I, 390f.
2. Frequently in "Poems about Baal and Anath" in James B. Pritchard, ed., *Ancient Near Eastern Texts* (Princeton, 1950) 129-142.
3. Edmund Schlink, *The Coming Christ and the Coming Church* (Philadelphia, 1968) 30f.
4. Claus Westermann, *The Praise of God in the Psalms* (Richmond, Va., 1965) 15.
5. In Num. 21:14 a quotation is given from an otherwise unpreserved source which bore the name, "The Book of the Wars of the Lord."
6. See especially the discussion by Gerhard von Rad, *Old Testament Theology* (New York, 1962) I, 17.
7. The RSV "be still" here is confusing, for different Hebrew words are employed in Exod. 14:14 and Ps. 46:10. To bring this out I have employed my own literal translation for Ps. 46:10.
8. In an attempt to capture this word-play in English the Jerusalem Bible renders: "But if you do not stand by me, you will not stand at all."
9. Franz Hesse, "The Evaluation and the Authority of Old Testament Texts," *Essays on Old Testament Hermeneutics*, ed. by Claus Westermann (Richmond, Va., 1963) 301.

93

10. Walther Zimmerli, *Old Testament Theology in Outline* (Atlanta, 1978) 20.

11. E. P. Sanders, *Paul and Palestinian Judaism* (Philadelphia, 1977) 138f.

12. Sadly I have forgotten where I heard this story, but this theme and the related one of the exaltation of penitence over piety are not uncommon. Consider, for example, the idea of a compartment in Paradise for "the penitents, who occupy a place which even a perfectly pious man cannot attain." Louis Ginzberg, *Legends of the Jews* (Philadelphia, 1942) I, 21.

13. Hans Walter Wolff, "The Kerygma of the Yahwist," *Vitality of Old Testament Traditions* (Atlanta, 1975) 53-55.

14. Wolff, "The Elohistic Fragments in the Pentateuch," *Vitality of Old Testament Traditions,* 74f.

15. von Rad, "Faith Reckoned as Righteousness," *The Problem of the Hexateuch and Other Essays* (New York, 1966) 125-130.

16. Jörg Jeremias, *Die Reue Gottes* (Neukirchen, 1975) 19-38.

17. von Rad, "The Beginnings of Historical Writings in Ancient Israel," *The Problem of the Hexateuch and Other Essays,* 201-204.

18. 1 Chron. 21:1—22:1 records a story of how the site for the temple altar was chosen as a result of its being the place at which a plague was stopped. Still, even this story does not deal with the city, just the altar location. The account of the capture of the city of David in 2 Sam. 5:6-9 does not even mention God.

19. Claus Westermann, *Isaiah 40–66* (Philadelphia, 1969) 43f.

20. Martin Noth, "The Laws in the Pentateuch: Their Assumptions and Meaning," *The Laws in the Pentateuch and Other Essays* (Philadelphia, 1967) 2-6.

21. *The Book of Concord: The Confessions of the Evangelical Lutheran Church,* trans. and edited by T. G. Tappert, in collaboration with J. Pelikan, R. H. Fischer and A. C. Piepkorn (Philadelphia, 1959) 112.

22. J. A. Sanders, "Torah," *Interpreter's Dictionary of the Bible* (Nashville, 1976), Supplementary Vol. 909.

23. Not just Jews, but the whole human race is involved in this rejection.

24. "Our every attempt to please God falls short of the mark. By the standards of the Law, of which the Ten Commandments are a classic summary, God expresses his just and loving expectations for his creation. And our failure to live up to these expectations reveals only our need for God's mercy and forgiveness." "What Lutherans Believe," an Evangelical Outreach pamphlet of the Division for Parish Services of the Lutheran Church in America.

25. *The Book of Concord,* 112.

26. Deut. 10:20, 11:22, 13:4, and 30:20.

27. Ps. 31:24, 33:18 and 22, 69:3, and 147:11.

28. Gen. 15:6, Exod. 14:31, Deut. 1:32, 2 Kings 17:14.

29. Vv. 9, 16, 17, 25, 28, 42, 49, 65, 74, 81, 89, 101, 105, 107, 114, 160, and 169.

30. See Ps. 119:38, 41, 50, 58, 76, 116, 133, 140 and 154.

31. See Deut. 27:15-26, esp. v. 26.

32. See Pss. 15 and 24:3-4 and Ezek. 18:5-9.

33. See 1 Kings 8:31-32 and Ezek. 18.

34. See, e.g., the "no pity" formula in Deut. 13:8.

35. von Rad, *Old Testament Theology,* II, 116-119.

36. Norman K. Gottwald, *Light to the Nations* (New York, 1959) 437f.

37. "Justification by works" according to the *Oxford English Dictionary,* s.v.

38. Heb. 8:6-13, Luke 22:20, and 1 Cor. 11:25 are the main references.

39. Exod. 34:6, 2 Chron. 30:9, Neh. 9:17 and 31, Pss. 86:15, 103:8, 111:4, and 145:8, Joel 2:13, and Jonah 4:2.

40. See, for instance, 2 Cor. 1:2 and 13:14.

41. Ronald M. Hals, "Luther and the First Commandment," *Interpreting Luther's Legacy,* ed. by Fred W. Meuser and Stanley D. Schneider (Minneapolis 1969) 2-13.

42. Jer. 2:9-13.